In my more than thirty yea  leading, and loving troops—I came ·tant element on the battlefield was t ıd sense of purpose—call it "the warrior soul." Boykin and Weber know that too, and this book makes it crystal clear. I highly recommend it.

—GEN. TOMMY FRANKS (RET.)
Former commander in chief
US Central Command

The Warrior Soul nails it. Ask any proven warrior where the battle is won or lost, and he'll likely point straight to his own heart. It takes a ton of heart to run to the guns. When the heart goes out of the warrior, the battle is over. This book is chock-full of the kind of soul-strengthening leadership principles that provide clarity in the midst of chaos and breed confidence under fire. Just the chapter "The Power of the Ten-Second Prayer" alone is worth the price of the book. Both Boykin and Weber are warriors of the heart who have made a difference on multiple fronts, and the principles in this book apply across the board to battles beyond physical combat.

—MAJ. GEN. GARY HARREL (RET.)
Former Delta Force commander
Special Operations Command
US Central Command

Jerry Boykin and Stu Weber are friends of mine and fellow warriors. They know gunfights, fear, anger, and the adrenaline rush of combat. In *The Warrior Soul* these two patriots capture the essential qualities, virtues, and values necessary to prevail in life's battles. Whether it is tracers, RPGs, and IEDs, or the calamity waiting where you go to work or when you walk in the front door at home, they have "been there, done that." This is a guidebook for all who wonder, "What do I do now?"

—LT. COL. OLIVER NORTH, USMC (RET.)
Host, *War Stories* on FOX News Channel

The hand of God has guided Stu and Jerry in their quest to "continue to serve." They are proven warriors who have survived, not unscathed, on the many battlefields of life, and here they share some of their most valued life lessons. *The Warrior Soul* is a handbook on how to check your spiritual/moral compass to stay on course. This book should be in the personal libraries of all warriors and leaders.

—COL. ROGER DONLON, US ARMY (RET.)
Green Beret, Republic of Vietnam
Medal of Honor, Republic of Vietnam

This book will stir the soul of any reader. Stu Weber and Jerry Boykin describe something worth dying for and a life worth living. Read *The Warrior Soul* and you will find your soul awakened to face this war zone we call planet Earth.

—MAJ. JEFF STRUECKER, US ARMY (RET.)
Winner, Best Ranger Competition
Multiple deployments with elite Seventy-Fifth Ranger Regiment
Notable role in Mogadishu, Somalia, and Black Hawk Down
Chaplain, pastor, author, national speaker

No theories. No quick solutions or shortcuts. Hard-hitting truth with genuine caring and compassion gained through decades of personal experience. If you are a warrior looking for answers, read this book. Then reread it.

—COL. SCOTT MCCHRYSTAL, US ARMY (RET.)
Infantry platoon leader, RVN
Multiple tours with the Eighty-Second Airborne Division
Former senior chaplain at the US Military Academy, West Point

THE WARRIOR SOUL

JERRY BOYKIN & STU WEBER

CHARISMA
HOUSE

Most CHARISMA HOUSE BOOK GROUP products are available at special quantity discounts for bulk purchase for sales promotions, premiums, fund-raising, and educational needs. For details, write Charisma House Book Group, 600 Rinehart Road, Lake Mary, Florida 32746, or telephone (407) 333-0600.

THE WARRIOR SOUL by Jerry Boykin and Stu Weber
Published by Charisma House
Charisma Media/Charisma House Book Group
600 Rinehart Road
Lake Mary, Florida 32746
www.charismahouse.com

Unless otherwise noted, all Scripture quotations are from the New American Standard Bible, copyright © 1960, 1962, 1963, 1968, 1971, 1972, 1973, 1975, 1977, 1995 by The Lockman Foundation. Used by permission. (www.Lockman.org)

Scripture quotations marked ESV are from the Holy Bible, English Standard Version. Copyright © 2001 by Crossway Bibles, a division of Good News Publishers. Used by permission.

Scripture quotations marked KJV are from the King James Version of the Bible.

Scripture quotations marked NIV are taken from the Holy Bible, New International Version®, NIV®. Copyright © 1973, 1978, 1984, 2011 by Biblica, Inc.™ Used by permission of Zondervan. All rights reserved worldwide. www.zondervan.com The "NIV" and "New International Version" are trademarks registered in the United States Patent and Trademark Office by Biblica, Inc.™

Cover design by Studio Gearbox
Design Director: Justin Evans

Visit the author's website at www.kingdomwarriors.net.

Library of Congress Cataloging-in-Publication Data:
Boykin, William G.
  The warrior soul / by Jerry Boykin and Stu Weber. -- First edition.
    pages cm
  Includes bibliographical references.
  ISBN 978-1-62998-016-4 (trade paper) -- ISBN 978-1-62998-017-1 (e-book)
  1. Conflict management--Religious aspects--Christianity. 2. Interpersonal relations--Religious aspects--Christianity. 3. Military ethics. 4. Soldiers--Psychology. I. Weber, Stu. II. Title.
  BV4597.53.C58B68 2016
  248.4--dc23
                                        2014041767

17 18 19 20 21 — 11 10 9 8 7 6
Printed in the United States of America

✯✯✯

To all Christians, men and women, who are
determined to "fight the good fight" (1 Tim.
6:12) to which our Lord has called us.

And to the soldiers, sailors, marines,
and airmen and women

of the armed forces of the United
States of America…

to all those, past and present, who've served,

and to all those who love them.

✯✯✯

Suffer hardship with me, as a good
soldier of Jesus Christ.
—2 TIMOTHY 2:3

✯✯✯

★★★

I have eaten your bread and salt,
I have drunk your water and wine,
The deaths ye died I have watched beside,
And the lives that ye led were mine.[1]

—RUDYARD KIPLING

★★★

I will sing to the LORD, for He is highly exalted....
The LORD is my strength and song....
The LORD is a warrior;
The LORD is His name....
Your right hand, O LORD, is majestic in power,
Your right hand, O LORD, shatters the enemy....
Who is like You, majestic in holiness,
Awesome in praises, working wonders?...
The LORD shall reign forever and ever.

—MOSES, EXODUS 15:1–3, 6, 11, 18

★★★

Blessed be the LORD, my rock,
Who trains my hands for war,
And my fingers for battle;
My lovingkindness and my fortress,
My stronghold and my deliverer,
My shield and He in whom I take refuge.

—DAVID, PSALM 144:1–2

★★★

✦ Contents ✦

UP FRONT!

A Personal Word From the Authors

BOYKIN AND WEBER here. Listen up. *War changed our lives!* War has a way of altering many things for many people. We might think first of the material damage caused in every war. For some it's the loss of houses, lands, or possessions. For others the damage is even more personal—the loss of limbs or other severe wounds. And for some there's the ultimate loss of life itself.

But beyond these obvious physical losses there are other changes. Oftentimes war has a profound *spiritual* impact upon people.

That's our story.

War sifts a soldier's belief system. The crucible of combat sorts our souls. It strips away the superficial elements of our lives and forces us to define what we *really* believe. Trivial concerns and pat answers evaporate like water on a summer sidewalk while that which feeds our innermost spirits is refined like gold. Up against the heat and horror of war, faith is tempered like the strongest of steel.

★★★

For me, Stu, the spiritual change began in the springtime on a hillside in the Dak Poko Valley. A member of the Fifth Special Forces Group, I was attached to the A-Team at Dak Pek, A-242, in Vietnam's Central Highlands. In early April 1970 the camp came under siege by multiple companies of two North Vietnamese regiments. It was there in the trauma and uncertainty that I first seriously considered the fact I might actually die in the red clay of a jungle half a world away from my roots. Death was no longer theoretical for me. In fact, it was a strong likelihood.

Unless you've experienced this yourself, you have no idea how facing real, literal, imminent death can alter the way you look at life. Thoughts that hadn't occurred to me for years suddenly crowded front and center.

Suddenly roots began to matter. The very real potential of dying at the ripe young age of twenty-four caused me to evaluate the long-abandoned spiritual roots of my childhood. After some months of examining afresh the claims of Jesus Christ—at a personal level I'd never before experienced—I concluded that Christ was indeed everything He claimed to be. I was drawn deeply to Him.

In order to know Him more authentically, I knew I had to know the Scriptures. So I made the difficult decision to resign my commission in order to attend seminary. I've been engaged in vocational ministry now for forty years.

War changed my life.

★★★

I, Jerry, took a different route. I served thirty-seven years as a professional soldier in the US Army's special operations community, and along the way I've had the privilege of leading some of the army's most elite soldiers.

During those decades I often found myself threatened with death in combat environments—and utterly dependent upon the living God. Looking back, I consider my life a testimony to what I call the power of a ten-second prayer. Whether it was the fireball of exploding aircraft at Desert One in the failed attempt to rescue the Americans held hostage in Tehran; or a .50-caliber round shredding my chest and arm in Grenada; or facing down Noriega in Panama; or chasing Pablo Escobar, Colombia's notorious drug lord; or the hot sting of mortar shrapnel in my shoulder in Mogadishu, Somalia—each time I've found my Lord faithful to answer my prayer.

Following my retirement from the military in 2007, I was ordained as a minister of the gospel of my Lord Jesus Christ. I consider that my greatest assignment, and one that I've been uniquely trained for by my experience as a soldier.

War changed my life.

★★★

This book represents our desire to impart to you some of the things we've learned in our personal experiences in the military and across all of life. We're confident you'll find the book engaging—a page-turner, as they say—but we didn't invest ourselves in this project of many months just to corral your interest or create a good read. Our strong desire is to introduce you to the concept of the warrior soul within you. You do have a warrior soul, you know!

Here is the reality, Christian—whether you realize it or not, you are engaged in a war. Life is a battle. Earth is a war zone. The people around you are walking wounded. And you are likely wounded too.

Just as a professional soldier is not merely the average citizen, so the committed Christian—a true spiritual warrior—is not merely the average believer.

True warriors are a determined lot. "Fighting the good fight" is no casual thing. Accordingly this book is not written for Christian laggards. It is not written for infants seeking milk. It is written for warriors. That means it is written for thinkers. Thinkers who take the call of Christ personally. And reflectively—carefully considering the application of these principles to their own actions. There's no room here for the weak-minded. Or the weak-souled. Be the best you can be—before God.

Don't look for spiritual pabulum, some easy-to-swallow Christian television tidbit. Eat the meat of the Word of God. Consume it in the presence of your fellow warriors. Find a local church (your warrior formation) that takes the Word seriously—not merely as a collection of platitudes but as a real, live battle manual meant to be read and understood, not emotionally hyped. Stick with the program, soldier. Never, never, never quit!

You are facing the very real "fiery darts" of the ultimate enemy, the evil one himself.

Every temptation to cheat is a bullet.

Every temptation to shade the truth is a bullet.

Every temptation to take unearned financial benefit is a bullet.

Every temptation to develop an illicit immoral relationship is a missile.

Every temptation to slight your King of kings is a major missile.

The activities and choices of everyday life are made on a *tactical* level. The fight is daily. The trajectory of your lifetime, however, is a *strategic* matter. Your tactical (daily) choices are made in light of the strategic (big picture) trajectory. Mission first. Live and die by your training in the finest warrior's manual ever written—the Word of God.

We also have a very personal hope—that this book will give to every reader a deeper and more personal respect, even love, for the warriors who have served in our nation's armed forces.

It is our desire, with God helping us, to give you the opportunity to discover and forge your own warrior soul. We hope this book plays some small part in reviving the warrior soul that God Himself put inside *you*.

Soldier on!

—JERRY BOYKIN AND STU WEBER

P.S. If you're going to read only one chapter of this book, make it the last one, chapter 13, "The Greatest Warrior Who Ever Lived."

AN IMPORTANT
NOTE TO READERS

WE RECOGNIZE THAT God has called every believing *man* and *woman* to be a spiritual warrior in His service. That being said and *firmly* believed by your authors, you will notice that most of the illustrations, stories, and examples used in the following pages will have something of a "male tone" to them.

This is in no way intended to diminish the role of our Lord's female warriors. It is the case for a couple of simple reasons: both of your authors are men, and most of their life experience has been in the company of men.

It's our hope that every warrior reading this book, whether male or female, will experience the soul-growing affirmation for which it was written.

Warr'-i-or. Webster defines the term *warrior* this way: "broadly: a person engaged in some struggle or conflict."[1] Here's what we want you to understand: We believe that "warrior" is, at its essential core, a gender-free term. Both men and women can be warriors. Indeed, both *should* be warriors. (In fact, boys and girls too should be budding warriors.) All human beings must be warriors to some degree. It is the nature of life on this struggling planet.

As you will soon read, your authors believe all of life is something of a struggle—a battle, if you will. Correspondingly, Earth is something of a war zone. Simply put, life is not easy. Even the good parts, such as love and marriage, for example, have their struggles. From birth to death, from paper cuts to politics, from the playground to the classroom, life is often a fight. From that first breath in the delivery room to that final gasp at life's end, we are all—males and females—involved in that struggle at multiple levels. In fact, the great apostle Paul, near the end of his days, summarized his entire lifetime as fighting "the good fight" (1 Tim. 6:12).

Soldier on.

Chapter 1

THE ORIGINAL UNCLE SAM

(and a Nephew and Niece or Two)

> We are building...morale—not on supreme
> confidence in our ability to conquer...not
> in reliance on things of steel and the super-
> excellence of guns...[but] on things infinitely
> more potent. We are building it on *belief*; for it is
> what men *believe* that makes them invincible.[1]
> • GEN. GEORGE C. MARSHALL •

WHAT MEN BELIEVE makes all the difference in the world. For America's revolutionary soldiers, that belief was *freedom*.

Brigadier General Hugh Percy was dumbstruck. He never imagined the colonials at Lexington and Concord would have the audacity to attack his British regulars, the finest infantry in the world. But before that historic day of battle was over, his contempt for the Americans had turned into a soldier's battlefield respect.

The next day, writing to another British general, he had this to say about the Americans: "Whoever looks upon them as an irregular mob, will find himself much mistaken"; indeed, "they have men amongst them who know very well what they are about." Percy noted their "perseverance and resolution," their "spirit of enthusiasm." And he recalled how "they advanced within 10 yds. to fire at me & other officers, tho' they were morally certain of being put to death themselves in an instant."[2]

I believe General Percy was describing our colonial soldiers at multiple levels. Yes, they knew something about frontier fighting tactics. But on a deeper level, at their core, they knew so much more. They were displaying an inner fire, as men who "know what they're about." They *got it*. These men had asked, "*Why?*"—and were willing to die for the answer. They were men who believed something and knew what they believed.

Spiritually Fit

You might call this the core of the warrior soul—a belief strong enough both to live for and die for.

And it's not just America's revolutionary warriors who "got it." I was seated in a stark room in Afghanistan with quite a number of young American soldiers of the twenty-first century. The commanding general of the US Army's Tenth Mountain Division stood in front of them. Apparently newly arrived, they were about to receive their first instructions from their two-star commander. His words were few, direct, and to the heart of soldiering. They went something like this: "I need three things from every one of you men. First, I need you to be physically fit. We need legs and lungs in this altitude. Second, I need you to be tactically fit. The man next to you depends on it for his life. Third, I need you to be spiritually fit. Everything depends on what you believe." The general went on to invite men to talk with him personally if they weren't sure what it meant to be spiritually fit.

America's revolutionary warriors believed in something: *freedom*. It showed up in the heat of every battlefield. It was the majestic core of their every thought—summarized in their Declaration of Independence. They determined to "live free or die." And that concept, encapsulated in the US Constitution, is at the center of the oath every American warrior still takes today upon enlistment.

Where do you get such men like those who shocked the British general at Lexington and Concord? They aren't born that way. Men don't come by it casually. Such men are built, shaped, taught, and trained. *Forged.* From the inside out.

It all begins in the soul, that unseen but deeply resident core. It's the inside that carries the outside. Ancient wisdom tells us that as a man thinks in his heart, so is he (Prov. 23:7). It's what a man believes that governs his behavior. *Warrior actions are derived from the warrior soul.* The best know it and nurture it.

And once you have it, it never leaves. The warrior soul does not weaken. Long after the body has broken down, the soul stands tall.

UNFADING

I want to introduce you now to a handful of such warrior souls. At center stage in this chapter you'll meet one of the Minutemen of the Revolutionary War. You'll also meet an elite Navy SEAL or two, along with their wives, magnificent women. And you'll meet a bronzed Bronze Age warrior, an iron man before there was an Iron Age.

All of them believed. And it showed on the battlefield.

You've no doubt heard the saying, "Old soldiers never die; they just fade away." If Douglas MacArthur didn't coin the phrase, he certainly made it walk on all fours. But I was never quite able to grasp its sentiment. I could see the "never die" part; a warrior who believes in something strong enough to actually give his life for it will live on in many grateful memories.

But "fade away"? That part never made much sense to me. It still doesn't.

A soldier's physical prowess certainly fades—we all experience that. But the heart—the core—doesn't fade. His bench press may not be as impressive as before, but that warrior soul keeps raising its tough old head, right to the end.

Most of the old soldiers I've known came close to dying more than once, and whatever it was inside them that made them true soldiers, it *never, ever* seemed to diminish—not even at the end, when their final breath expired. In fact, "fading" (or rolling over or lying down) was pretty much out of the equation for them.

They just didn't have a "stop" switch.

And for good reason.

How often have we seen Christian men and women stop? Now, of course, we would never use the word *stop* or *quit*. No, we're more subtle than that. But we often say things like, "We just need an extended break." Or, "Last fall was such a busy season, we're going to step back for a while." Or the more apparently pious, "…besides, it would be good for someone else to have a shot at it." The point is this: before you stop, make sure it's your Lord giving the orders and not your flesh. Our days are numbered, and so far as I know, we were not issued a stop switch either. The enemy certainly never rests.

The Difference

What men believe makes a difference. Ask members of Delta Force. Or SEAL Team Six. Or ask Adam Brown.

Adam gave his life for you and me in March 2010 in Afghanistan. When members of his elite SEAL team described him afterward, a single theme repeatedly emerged. Adam had no "fear bone." He had "no fear and no temperance regulator."

Adam's mission on that fateful March day was to have been his last. He was due to rotate home. He'd already done it all—he'd seen the elephant of combat multiple times and fought alongside the best. In fact, he was the best of the best.

A lesser man would have been finished long before. After all, Adam had already lost an eye, and his dominant eye at that. He was medically qualified for a disability pension and could have been discharged. No way! No fading away here. Adam drove on. The guy had a glass eye installed, complete with a pupil displaying an Arkansas Razorback icon (his favorite college team).

Adam never quit—he just retrained his remaining eye to shoot better than most men shoot with their dominant eye.

He once got the ends of several fingers crushed and severed when his Humvee rolled three times. A teammate picked up the pieces, and a surgeon later reattached them—not quite as good as new, since the nerves never recovered their sense of feel. But that was no problem for Adam—stiff stumps were better than nothing. Drive on.

And the warrior went back to battle.[3] (To view a video of Adam's story, visit the NRA Life of Duty website at www.nralifeofduty.tv/ adambrown.)

Are you ever tempted to quit? Of course you are. We all are from time to time. And there is a place for "spiritual R&R," but it has limits. Because the battle never stops. It always rages on.

SHARED BY WIFE AND FAMILY

While you're watching those videos about Adam, listen to his young children describe their daddy—and have some Kleenex on hand. *Whew!* Adam's warrior soul gave his kids an example to follow. Listen carefully as well to Adam's young widow, the mother of those children. Kelley Brown is a woman with a warrior soul all her own. Hear the strength in this magnificent woman as she rehearses the loss of her best friend and life partner. Kelley loved her husband with a passion.

Prior to their wedding Adam's own father wasn't so sure Kelley knew what she was getting into by marrying this driven man so full of energy and a sense of mission. But Kelley would find it out for herself, and she would love him all the more. She knew full well that her husband's calling regularly took him to knock on death's door, and not lightly. So she determined that her warrior soul would strengthen his. They were a great warrior team.

Kelley's warrior soul sustained her in the darkest of days and longest of months following Adam's death. Her soul was strong enough and wise enough to sort through the enormous loss of her husband. A full year after Adam's death Kelley could say with an astonishing resolve in her heart that she had no regrets, and she and Adam would do it the same way again. Somehow this very feminine warrior knew that anything less would dishonor her husband.

Only sixteen months after Adam's death Kelley would be called upon to stand beside many of her close friends, now widows themselves. Adam's teammates, all members of SEAL Team Six—the very same men who had honored Adam at his memorial service by jumping off the bridge into Lake Hamilton, Arkansas, the previous spring—followed him in death when their CH-47 Chinook helicopter was hit by a Taliban RPG (rocket-propelled grenade). Also killed that day were ten other American special operations personnel, five Army National Guard crewmen, and eight Afghan military personnel. They'd been pulled together for a quick reaction force on a mission to rescue a US Army Ranger unit heavily engaged in the Tangi Valley of Wardak Province, Afghanistan.

One of the SEALs killed in that crash was Aaron Vaughn. Aaron too was a man of strong belief—and it made all the difference for him and his family.

Two days after the crash Aaron's grieving widow and parents were interviewed on national television.[4] Billy Vaughn spoke of his son's love for God, his family, and his country. And the elder Vaughn wanted to make one point very clear: his son's sacrifice grew directly out of his son's beliefs. "He felt," Vaughn told the reporter, "and so did the other members of his team, that the very existence of our republic is at stake, and because of that, Aaron was willing to give his life."

Aaron's mother, Karen Vaughn, added, "I am most proud of Aaron's humility and nobility, but more than anything I'm most proud of the way he loved God and how important his faith was to him....He believed America could be great again, and he fought for the America he grew up in."

Kimberly Vaughn, Aaron's widow, choked back tears as she spoke of the heritage their children would derive from their father's legacy: "They will take away his love for Christ. They will take away his strength and his love for this country. And they will know what an amazing man he is...*was*."

For the children of both Adam Brown and Aaron Vaughn, their young warrior souls are actually growing in the wake of their daddies' sacrifice. That's what true warriors do; they nurture those coming along. They carefully pass the baton of cause and courage to the next generation.

So it is with the warrior soul. There's no stop switch.

A Minuteman Who Refused to Fade Away

As we step forward in our journey to better understand the warrior soul, let me acquaint you with the most famous patriot soldier you've likely never heard of. This tough old buzzard should have stopped, even died, a dozen times. And he almost did. He was a living legend in his own day, so I suppose you could say in his old age he'd tried to just fade away on his farm surrounded by scores of grateful descendants. But it wasn't to be. When his country was in trouble, his warrior soul couldn't resist responding—even when he was in his eighties!

This reminds me of a stack of letters on General Boykin's desk at the JFK Special Warfare Center (SWC) at Fort Bragg, North Carolina—the training center and fountainhead for all US Army Green Berets. The letters poured in immediately after 9/11. They were from retired Special Forces soldiers, and their contents were all variations of the same theme: "I may have done my time and retired, but I want to be in this fight. And since I'm too old to run the rugged mountains of Afghanistan and to keep up with today's young troopers, how about if I come back to the Special Warfare Center and relieve your staff and cadre? I know you must be itching to get in the fight." You have to love that attitude: *Hey, I'm a little older and slower than I used to be, but I still have plenty of fire in my belly, and I'd like to join the cause!*

I can see Samuel Whittemore writing a letter like that.[5] This old soldier, long retired, loved working his fields near the town of Menotomy in colonial Massachusetts, about seven miles out from Boston. There was something about wrestling a living from the soil that appealed to Sam.

Born around 1695, he'd served as a captain of the King's Dragoons. He was already fifty when he fought the French at the Fortress of Louisburg in Nova Scotia in 1745. There he acquired his favorite war trophy, a saber he'd taken from a French officer. When asked about it, Sam, without elaboration, simply explained that the Frenchman had "died suddenly."

When the hostilities ended, he bought the farm at Menotomy, built a house with his own hands, and settled his family there. When war kicked up again with the French, Sam volunteered, and at age sixty-four he was sent to help recapture Louisburg. The following year he was part of General Wolfe's expedition that took Quebec from the French.

Later, nearing seventy, he fought in the frontier Indian wars. He came home this time astride a much finer horse than he'd left with, and he now owned a brace of pistols whose previous owner had also, in Sam's words, "died suddenly."

For Sam, back in Menotomy, life was good. Having traveled far and wide, survived multiple combat deployments, and fought against enemies of varying stripes and tactics, in his senior years he was now loving life and basking in the admiration of his wife, his children, and his many grandchildren and great-grandchildren.

But in the spring of 1775 Sam could see storm clouds gathering, and he was deeply concerned about threats to his freedom, both foreign and domestic. Freedom was what Sam had always fought for, and he found living in freedom to be a glorious way of life. Freedom's song hummed in his soul. He openly stated that he wanted his descendants to live in a free land where they could govern and be governed by their own laws and not have their lives dictated by a king on the other side of the earth.

Sam knew well that freedom is never free. That's why, like many of his countrymen, he was agitated by the current political climate—the posturing, the scare tactics, and what he regarded as pure bullying. His free way of life was threatened; freedom's enemies had become blatantly aggressive. And he wasn't going to take it anymore.

The pulse of his warrior heart was pounding with a familiar vigor.

Other, lesser men would have considered it time to sit back, relax, and enjoy the flight. After all, Sam had "done his part." He'd earned his stripes, paid his dues.

Time to fade away? Not on your life! Certainly not on Sam's watch.

Sam's "aged" soldiering is a model for all of us. The guy never quit! Believer, if you are alive, you are still a spiritual warrior. You are still serving. There is no "time out." There is no "retirement." Until God calls you home, you're officially on active duty. One prominent Christian preacher, in his own senior years, said that much of his ministry was spent traveling the country, trying to motivate Christian retirees to get off the golf course and back into the battle. Let's stay in the fight. Every day. Every hour.

AGED TO PERFECTION

April 19, 1775—arguably the most important day in American history—was a fine spring day. The air was clear, and the smell of freshly turned soil filled the nostrils of eighty-year-old Samuel Whittemore as he breathed deeply of freedom.

You know what happened that glorious day. A corps of hundreds of British regulars—the world's finest professional soldiers at the time—had been given secret orders to march out from Boston and capture colonial militia supplies at Concord, eighteen miles up the road. (It was an early attempt at gun control on American soil.) But the Minutemen wouldn't give up their guns. The colonials got word of the British operation and made their own plans. As the Redcoats' advance element headed out, they made contact with Captain John Parker's Minutemen at Lexington, armed and ready.

The veteran Parker had prepared his grim-faced company with these famous words from his warrior soul: "If they mean to have a war, let it begin here." By early morning eight freedom-loving Americans lay dead on the green. Six of the eight were three fathers and their three sons. So it is in every freedom-loving generation: the ones who "get it" pass it on.

Leaving Lexington somewhat bruised by the colonials' resistance, the British companies moved on toward Concord. The countryside was abuzz. Minutemen, contrary to the common myth of their being a bunch of disorganized, spontaneous rabble, responded to their sophisticated alert system of organized riders.

Meeting the British regulars at Concord was a large American force that just kept growing. They fought hard. The Redcoats, over-whelmed in this deadly clash, fell back.

Their road back to Boston would take them through Sam Whittemore's hometown of Menotomy. And Sam had decided they were going to get a bellyful.

Over his eighty years the warrior soul in Sam's chest had matured to the finest of quality and the sharpest of edges. His warrior soul had never been more sharply honed. Like a fine wine, this original "Uncle Sam" had aged to perfection—at least as a soldier if not a farmer.

Having taken strong root in a man's chest, the warrior soul never leaves, never quits, never surrenders—and certainly never runs from a just fight. No matter the odds.

Octogenarian or not, Sam Whittemore would do his part again.

The old soldier knew what to do and where to go. He had methodically loaded his trusted musket and his already famous set of dueling pistols. He stuffed his well-traveled pack with more powder and ball, strapped on his previously captured French saber, told his family what he was up to, then ordered them to remain inside until he returned.

Then he walked to a position he'd selected near a tavern, behind a rock wall at a strategic intersection that the British would have to pass on their return to Boston. Records suggest that a number of other militiamen tried to talk Sam out of the vulnerable position. But Sam wasn't out that day to avoid a fight. He intended to pick one. His chosen spot gave him a clear view of the road from Lexington. And as the ensuing hours would demonstrate, it placed the old soldier directly in the path of the approaching 47th British Regiment and their flankers.

The greatest moment in Sam Whittemore's life was about to unfold.

FINAL STAND

As the British pushed ahead, the fighting in Menotomy was particularly fierce, from house to house and cellar to cellar. Death came to many; some were even reportedly shot by the British after being taken prisoner.

While the shooting got closer, Sam held his fire. Minutemen on both sides of him were firing their muskets, then they'd sprint away to reload. But not Sam. Waiting for the right moment, when the enemy was almost on top of him, he stood up and fired his musket, dropping one British regular in midstep. Sam then jumped out from behind the wall and fired off both his fine pistols, killing one Redcoat immediately and mortally wounding another.

That kind of opposition draws a lot of attention. Fire draws fire. With no time to reload his weapons, Sam drew his saber and "flailed away at the cursing, enraged Redcoats who now surrounded him."[6] Think of it: most of those British soldiers would have been less than half his age.

One of the regulars shot Sam point-blank in the face, tearing away half his cheek. The .69-caliber ball knocked him to the ground. Dazed, he rose, still trying to fight, but was again knocked down by a musket butt and bayoneted thirteen times by the vengeful Redcoats.[7]

The aftermath has been described this way:

When the last Britisher had left the scene and was far enough for them to come out in safety, the villagers who had seen Whittemore's last stand walked slowly toward the body. To their astonishment, he was still alive and conscious—and still full of fight! Ignoring his wounds, he was feebly trying to load his musket for a parting shot at the retreating regiment.[8]

Using a door as a makeshift stretcher, the townsmen carried Whittemore into the nearby tavern, where a doctor "stripped away Sam's torn, bloody clothing and was aghast at his many gaping bayonet wounds, the other numerous bruises and lacerations, and his horrible facial injury." The doctor "remarked that it was useless to even dress so many wounds, since Whittemore could not possibly survive for very long." But Whittemore's neighbors "persuaded the reluctant doctor to do his best.... When the bandaging was finally finished, old Sam was tenderly carried back to his home to die surrounded by his grieving family."[9]

To die?

Not quite!

That old warrior thought differently. Sam survived—and went on to live another eighteen years.

When later asked if he regretted his losses that day—injuries that left him lame and disfigured—Sam responded, "I would take the same chance again."[10]

I guess he still wasn't bothering to fade away.

In fact, I'm guessing Sam felt more alive than ever, and more eager than ever to sacrifice himself for freedom. There was an oft-heard maxim that circulated among Green Berets in Vietnam: "You have never lived till you've almost died. For those who've fought for it, freedom has a flavor the protected will never know." That flavor was something Sam cherished, deep in his warrior soul.

Samuel Whittemore eventually died of natural causes at age ninety-eight. He was survived by 185 direct descendants—and he was especially proud to know that every single one of them was living as a free American.[11]

Who We Are, Each One

So what's the lesson Sam would love for us to learn? Maybe something like this: You're just one person. But you *are* one person. Make a difference! Give yourself away to right principles and right values, deeply held. Believe. Then behave accordingly.

Sam Whittemore was just one American. He was never numbered among our nation's Founding Fathers. He didn't get to sign the Declaration of Independence or help draft the US Constitution. He didn't do the "big" things, but he made those things possible because he was America's greatest asset—a sacrificing, freedom-loving citizen-soldier. He and his ilk are the most critical factor in this battle—a common soldier with a "never quit" attitude. How about you? Do you view yourself as a kingdom warrior, following Christ's directives in this spiritual conflict on planet Earth?

Where do we find such men as Sam? That's a good question, but there's another that's more fundamental: *Where do such men get such a warrior soul?* If the warrior soul is something that's built, shaped, taught, and trained, how does that training and shaping happen? What kind of elements are required?

Which begs an even deeper issue: *Just what is the warrior soul? What are the essential elements?*

Glad you asked! That's what this book is about. And we're going to frame the answer around a conversation between two other old warriors, like Sam Whittemore, with lifetimes of military experience. One of them laid out the elements of the warrior soul in a campfire conversation before the next day's battle—and we get to listen in.

The warrior soul is a driven soul. What drives it?

Read on.

Chapter 2

LIFE IS A BATTLE, EARTH IS A WAR ZONE

And We're All Soldiers

The art of war is of vital importance....matter
of life and death, a road either to safety or to
ruin...under no circumstances can it be neglected.[1]
• SUN TZU, THE ART OF WAR •

T HIS IS A book by soldiers, to soldiers, for soldiers. And remember this: every single living, breathing human being—yes, including you—is a soldier.

Stick with me here. *Every man and every woman, every boy and every girl—every single person is in a battle.* We may not wear a uniform, do physical training every morning, eat in a mess hall, or dodge actual bullets for a living. But we're in a war, and a very crucial one. It's a war that will determine our quality of life, both in this world and in the real world to come. Two overriding motifs appear everywhere across the pages of Holy Scripture: a battle and a party. *This life is a battle. Eternity is a celebration.*

Just take a good look around you. We live in a war zone. That's not cute talk or just a metaphor. It's a reality. Walk into any room full of people, and you'll find a room full of pain, full of wounds. Oh, it may not look like a war zone. Most likely it even feels quite comfortable—*on the outside.* Beautiful people in a beautiful building wearing beautiful clothing surrounded by beautiful friends—how could such a room be filled with pain? But *on the inside,* deep within our own souls, when we slow down long enough to think about it, we realize life's a struggle.

Did I say *struggle*? That may be a tad too soft. It's more like a raging conflict, with all of planet Earth as the war zone.

If you look closely enough, you'll see this war's casualties everywhere, not only in your own life and home but next door too. Every home and family is something of a "listening post" in this enormous war. Sometime back in another book, *Spirit Warriors*, I (Stu) recorded some of the battlefield inventory—badly wounded warriors and scorched earth—in the tiny little suburban neighborhood where my wife and I raised our family for over twenty years.

I had written: "It's a middle-class neighborhood lined with respectable homes, shaded by mature trees, and occupied by your typical workday families. No ghetto. No gangs. It's actually a very desirable place to live."[2]

My inventory didn't have to delve too deeply, however, before it took a darker turn. In my mind, sitting at my desk at home, I simply surveyed the pain within half a dozen homes immediately surrounding ours. I didn't interview anyone; I just took stock of the most obvious wounds everybody knew about. Right next door our neighbor was dying of cancer. Up the street a ways a young teenager had committed suicide. Across the way a little family was aching over a son's sexual orientation. Down the road a home was missing a father because he was in prison. Another home was facing up to incest and sexual abuse charges. And another was dealing with the fallout of attempted murder.

The cumulative effect left me stunned. I'd known about each of these things as they happened along the way, but I'd never actually tried to add them up. The war was worse than I realized.

If you'll do the same exercise, you'll feel the concussion and smell the cordite of this spiritual war all around us. Life's a battle. Earth's a war zone.

WHY? WHAT'S WRONG?

Not long ago I sat in our church auditorium surrounded by more than a thousand mourners. One of our choice youngsters, barely twenty-one years old, had left us. He died of a self-inflicted bullet wound to the head. Judging by the audience, his circle of friends consisted of those who were young, vigorous, and full of energy.

A video was shown about his life—full of smiles, parties, boating, motorcycling, and lots of adventure. But for those in the church auditorium that day, those memories were smothered by something else. You could have cut the depression with a knife. It was more than the understandable discouragement at the untimely death of a friend. It was a reflective silence. People were asking themselves, "What's going on here? How could something like this happen?"

No, it was no accident. But it was certainly a mind-numbing tragedy. Human beings, it seems, kill themselves with a little more frequency with each passing day. The rooms of our lives are filled with pain. Battle casualties. Walking wounded.

Maybe you can't hear the moaning at the moment. But if every person you met was able to drop his cultural camouflage and be brutally honest with you, you'd hear pain, bruises, scars, and some kind of wound in every heart. Human disappointment is a universal reality.

From paper cuts to roadside bombs, from children falling off tricycles to parents falling out of love, it's all part of life's battles.

Ultimately all human pain and disappointment—yes, *all*—is traceable to a single source: the adversary of our souls. Satan is his name; destruction is his game. And he's so good at it, we all have holes in our hearts, and our planet is torn to shreds.

Earth is a battlefield—a fight site between God and Satan, good and evil, right and wrong, life and death, heaven and hell. Earth is a war zone full of smoke and anguish and the disorientation and shock of constant battle. Call it the fog of war. This battlefield is crisscrossed by wandering, stumbling, wounded human beings, deeply hurt and confused. And their only hope for recovery is in the battle plan of God—the covenants and promises of the Bible, the soldier's ultimate field manual.

The one historical constant on this planet is war. In Cormac McCarthy's western novel *Blood Meridian,* an old judge articulates the constant and universal nature of war on our planet when he says, "It makes no difference what men think of war....War endures. As well ask men what they think of stone. War was always here. Before man was, war waited for him."[3]

Long before that old judge noticed it, Jesus made the same thing clear:

> You will be hearing of wars and rumors of wars. See that you are not frightened, for those things must take place, but that is not yet the end. For nation will rise against nation, and kingdom against kingdom....But all these things are merely the beginning.
> —MATTHEW 24:6–8

The warfare theme so pervades Scripture that the Bible's first hint of the Messiah-Christ reveals Him as a wounded warrior. The description—in Genesis 3:15—pictures Jesus shedding His blood (wounded on the heel); in the process He deals the devil a mortal wound to the head.

Flip over to Revelation, and the last picture in Scripture of this same Jesus shows Him as a victorious commander in chief astride a great war horse, wearing a blood-splattered robe and carrying a sword that will both initiate and conclude the actual "war to end all wars." (See Revelation 19:11–21.) John the Apostle shares a glimpse of this with us: "And I saw heaven opened, and behold, a white horse, and He who sat on it is called Faithful and True, and in righteousness He judges and wages war" (Rev. 19:11).

Until then—until that hour when all the enemies of God and of righteousness are finally destroyed—life here will always be war.

Is it any wonder then that the Bible, our field manual for life, is replete with the vocabulary of war? It's all there—attacks, wounds, blood, sacrifice, swords, battles, victories. One of Christianity's greatest theologians, Saint Augustine, famously pointed out that the correct and reasonable purpose of war is peace.[4] Indeed, Christ will be the ultimate victor—but there will be no real peace until it's delivered by the Prince of Peace Himself.

THE REAL CONFRONTATION

Life is war. Sometimes it's as physical and vicious as our conflicts in Vietnam and Afghanistan. But even in physical combat war is spiritual. Sometimes war is external, waged with guns and bullets; sometimes it's political, fought over principles and philosophies; sometimes it's internal, against temptations and desires. But whether external or internal, it's always—*always, always, always*—spiritual at its core.

It's no good talking about a warrior soul until we've grappled with this reality.

The problem, however, is that most of us twenty-first-century Americans walk around as though we're headed for Disneyland. *Hey, be happy!* And we increase our vulnerability and lose our situational awareness by numbing ourselves with activities or substances. Objectively speaking, the evidence for this conflict might be inescapable; yet most of us still stubbornly avoid a realistic perspective about it.

Imagine a man talking animatedly into his cell phone, heedless of his surroundings, as he strolls into a minefield. That's the intensity of what we're talking about here.

My wife, Linda, and I are blessed to have ten grandchildren now. I think often and long about the world these little troopers are going to inherit. Little Number Ten is not even two years old yet. He's toddling around in a world bordered by his mother's arms, his father's shoulders, and his siblings' loving care. But before long he will be in for a rather rude awakening. This is a tough old world, and it's not only getting tougher all the time; it's actually beginning to tear itself apart. The constant chatter about the economy, government corruption and lawlessness, and the rise of Islamic terrorism are only examples (far-reaching to be sure) of our nation's alarming disintegration. As you well know, our world's *serious* problems are legion.

I've often thought that the first thing we communicate to every young child ought to be something honest like, "Welcome to the war, kid; grab your weapons and join the fight." Of course, we want every boy and girl to enjoy the innocence of a protected childhood. But I also believe every home is to raise that child with a growing, maturing "situational awareness" of the very real spiritual war zone in which he or she now lives. *Don't play in the street, kids; don't talk to strangers; and don't ignore the very real impact of the everyday reality in this spiritual warfare.*

I described it this way in a previous book, *Spirit Warriors*:

> Like tremors after an earthquake, these battles and skirmishes are scattered far and wide, experienced differently by a wide variety of people....Individual human beings are often caught out in the open, trapped in a cross fire of a battle that is much larger than they are prone to realize....Its explosive nature is readily visible all around us. Divorce. Child abuse. Epidemic addictions—alcohol, drugs, sex. Violent crime. Incredible dishonesty at the highest levels of government and culture....Like any battlefield, life is filled with confusion. Loud noises, chaos, the smell of explosives, and shock after shock after shock. It's downright dangerous.[5]

So what do we do about living in this war zone? For that rare man or woman who recognizes this truth about life, it begs a question. *How do I win?* How do I not only survive, but how do

I actually impact the battle's outcome? What's the key to winning this all-out, ever-present war?

Glad you asked. Let's let the professor answer.

Right Makes Might

Some years ago Victor Davis Hanson, a highly regarded classicist and military historian associated with Stanford University, wrote a book titled *The Soul of Battle*. Hanson focused on key military campaigns won against seemingly invincible foes in three significant wars—the Peloponnesian Wars of ancient Greece, the American Civil War, and World War II. He concluded that the winning armies, without exception, consisted of warriors driven more by conviction, principles, and values than by trust in technology and firepower.[6]

In other words, *what carried the day in each campaign was not weaponry but people*—more specifically, people who "knew what they were about," to recall General Percy's words about Lexington and Concord.

The dust cover of Hanson's book summarizes the questions he tackles inside: "Why do men fight? What motivates an ordinary citizen to burn and kill? What, in the end, motivates an army to win?" By examining "three incredible stories—the sagas of history's greatest marches," Hanson comes up with surprising answers:

> Each story involves a democratic army pulled together on short notice, which marched deep into enemy territory to overthrow a government whose morality was fundamentally repugnant to its own. Each army stunned the world by covering many miles and capturing huge numbers of its demoralized foes. In all three cases...conviction (more than firepower) made the difference against long odds.[7]

Hanson's conclusion has far-reaching consequences in our conviction-less times: *right makes might*.

These troops truly *believed* in morality, principles, values, and freedom. Hanson demonstrates conclusively that "halfhearted wars are rarely won."[8] No good soldier can fight with half a heart. It's the warrior soul that prevails, a soul nurtured on right versus wrong, freedom versus slavery.

Right makes might. While most of the world has historically sought to convince itself that he with the biggest guns pulls off the biggest victory, time and time again it's the little guy who slays the giant—because he "knows what he's about."

THE LARGE REALITIES

Nowhere is this theme more overt than in the Old Testament story of David and Goliath. The giant showed up in full battle array with implements of war large enough to shatter and shred any ten men foolish enough to face him. His helmet and coat of mail weighed over a hundred pounds. He wore a helmet, breastplate, and leggings of bronze, and he carried a javelin fitted with a spearhead weighing fifteen pounds. André the Giant couldn't have carried Goliath's handkerchief.

David, on the other hand, showed up with five rocks and a leather sling. Goliath talked big: "Come out here, kid! I'll give your flesh to the dogs and birds for their evening snack." But David talked much bigger. The original "young gun" put it straight to the bully, speaking in large realities instead of schoolyard taunts. David "knew what he was about." Listen to the kid's words to Goliath:

> You come to me with sword, spear, and javelin, but I come to you in the name of the LORD of Heaven's Armies—the God of the armies of Israel, whom you have defied. Today the LORD will conquer you, and I will kill you and cut off your head. And then I will give the dead bodies of your men to the birds and wild animals, and the whole world will know that there is a God in Israel! And everyone assembled here will know that

the LORD rescues his people, but not with sword and spear. This is the LORD's battle, and he will give you to us!

—1 SAMUEL 17:45-47, NLT

By the way, you might want to spend some lengthy time in this passage (and many others like it), where you find the Bible to be wonderfully frank. Most of us can recall a few Bible stories from the little purple-haired ladies and their flannelgraphs in vacation Bible school. But reading the Bible today—as an adult, and with at least a vague familiarity with the original languages—I realize we didn't hear the whole truth in Sunday school. I'm sure our teachers were trying to be age sensitive, but later on, when I ran up against life's horrors—especially in Vietnam—I tended to discount Scripture as failing to face life straight on, to deal with the bad as well as the good. Well, I was wrong about that, and I'm so pleased today to honor the sheer fearless transparency of Scripture.

For example, take the chapter that immediately follows the David and Goliath story. We're presented with quite a scene there in verses 17–27 of 1 Samuel 18. Plotting to get David killed on a battlefield, King Saul promises to give his daughter Michal to David in marriage. But of course there's a catch. David, without resources worthy of such a marriage, must prove himself. Saul informs him that the bride-price will be the foreskins of a hundred Philistines. Think about it: How do you collect foreskins? By stripping the dead bodies of enemy soldiers and mutilating their most private parts. (And this is about 2,300 years before *Braveheart*!)

The Bible describes David's response to Saul's crazy offer. Keep in mind, this is David, the guy God calls "a man after My heart" (Acts 13:22). The Bible records David's response to Saul's nutty, seemingly suicidal proposition: "David was *delighted to accept* the offer" (1 Sam. 18:26, NLT).

As we follow him into action, David, in effect, says to Saul, "I'll take your bet and raise you double":

> David rose up and went, he and his men, and struck down
> *two hundred men* among the Philistines. Then David brought
> their foreskins, and they gave them in full number to the king,
> that he might become the king's son-in-law. So Saul gave him
> Michal his daughter for a wife.
>
> —1 SAMUEL 18:27

Yes, the story is impacted by much of the culture of the ancient Near East, as well as by God's covenant with Israel. Circumcision was a sign and a signature identifying Israel as a family specially marked by God Himself. But none of that spiritual transcendence dilutes the sheer graphic horror of that battlefield. And this "circumcision" of the "uncircumcised" took place in a day long before Cutco and gunnysacks were available for David's use. One need say no more.

Though perhaps one should say just a little more. Let me put it this way: *the Bible doesn't mince words*. It doesn't hide anything, not even the "earthy" sides, to include the actual sins of its own heroes—such as David's adultery with Bathsheba. It puts it all right out there for the reader to sort out under the guidance of the Holy Spirit. As one writer said, "There is more to the Bible than Jesus petting lambs"; Scripture, he continues, is often "refreshingly shocking in its contradictions to the tame, Americanized version of the Christian faith."[9] Let me quote more from this observer:

> War is never glorified in Scripture, but neither is it shied away from. An honest assessment of the Bible would force us to conclude God had no intention of shielding us from the sorrowful acts of violence that men are capable of. It does us well not to tame the Word to fit our notions of what it should say but to examine all its gory detail in order to grasp the true depravity of man and the desperate need for redemption. David's warriors were content to do the "dirty work" that men so often forsake in our time: standing in the gap for what is right, overcoming their own destructive tendencies, and being

loyal to the point of death. These "Mighty Men" (of David) may or may not have been spiritual giants like Moses or Paul, but the Bible is effusive in its praise for their courage and deeds....David's life was continuous warfare of one kind or another...much of what we can understand of him is shaped by his war years.[10]

HEART BELIEF

OK, back to young David, as he embarks on his "continuous warfare" by facing Goliath in the Valley of Elah. Here's the point: the young kid acknowledged the giant had all the technology. He tipped his hat, so to speak, to Goliath's heavy-duty, sophisticated armor. But then he let the oversized soldier know straight up that he, the kid, had something much more—a heart full of ultimate belief in a sovereign God.

Let's call it *believing in a transcendent cause*. It's the first ingredient of the warrior soul—belief in something (in David's case, *Someone*) much larger than meets the eye. An invisible reality, if you will. A moral value. An abiding principle. A sustaining faith.

For David that transcendent cause was decidedly theological. No one could deny that reality. And if a person will have "ears to hear" (to quote the greater Son of David, Jesus, from Matthew 11:15) plus the integrity to recognize US history for what it is, he'll recognize a similar reality in the founding of these United States of America.

That was certainly what drove our own American Revolution and our nation's founding leaders: convictions, principles, values—more specifically and overtly, decidedly theological notions at that!

Consider the national birth certificate of the United States, *the* founding document of this nation: "We hold these truths to be self-evident, that all men are created equal, that they are endowed by their Creator with certain unalienable Rights."[11] Our founders believed human equality and human rights to be so utterly ultimate and true that they're "self-evident." It was, as I've heard several pundits put it, a "wonderfully Jeffersonian way of saying, 'Any fool can get this!'"

The Declaration of Independence affirms three important truths:

1. We're *created* beings…not self-formed primordial mud.

2. We're created as people, free and *equal*; no hereditary big shots here.

3. Our Creator has granted us *certain unalienable rights*. Our rights as free citizens of these United States are not derived from the Capitol or the White House or anywhere else in Washington, DC. Our rights are actually divinely given—*"endowed"* by the ultimately Transcendent One.

That defining statement from our defining document is a wonderfully idealistic, spiritual, and religious notion—clearly theological at its root and core. Here's the point: *it's what the warrior believes in his heart that drives him.* I can't overemphasize this. It's the very soul of battle and that which most potently impacts the battlefield.

That's why Napoleon would insist, "Even in war, moral power is to physical as three parts out of four."[12] The sword is ruled by the spirit. All of life, and all of war, is *spiritual* at its root. It's what we *believe* that drives us. What the warrior carries in his chest—in his soul—is what carries the day.

That explains David's battle buddy, Jonathan. When Israel had been stripped of all military hardware (only two large swords were left in the entire kingdom), Jonathan could say to his armor bearer, "Hey, let's take a little run up toward this Philistine outpost of six hundred troops outside Gibeah." Here was his reasoning: "Perhaps the LORD will help us, for nothing can hinder the LORD. He can win a battle whether he has many warriors or only a few!" (1 Sam. 14:6, NLT).

Jonathan and his comrade scaled those cliffs, faced off with the twenty Philistines who confronted them, and killed every one of them. And this was after those soldiers watched the two Israelites scale the cliff right in front of them! Odds of ten to one were overcome by Jonathan's belief in the ultimate transcendent cause, God Himself. When the sun set that day, all twenty Philistine bodies lay dead in about half an acre. Meanwhile panic overwhelmed the entire Philistine garrison, and they "beat feet" out of there. As Scripture says, "The vast army of Philistines began to melt away in every direction" (1 Sam. 14:16, NLT). Two guys, knowing what they were about and believing to the core what they believed, had sent packing the entire Philistine outposts of hundreds of battle-hardened soldiers.

FOR FREEDOM

Not surprisingly, the soul of battle has shown itself among our warriors in our most recent war, the so-called Global War on Terror(ists)—the parenthesis is mine. The Strategic Studies Institute of the US Army War College has studied our soldiers fighting in this war. In their report titled *Why They Fight: Combat Motivation in the Iraq War,* they noted how many soldiers "were motivated by idealistic notions. Liberating the people and bringing freedom to Iraq were common themes."[13]

What it takes to win a war is a soul of spiritual steel. What it takes to win any war—physical or spiritual—is *the warrior soul.*

So let's brush off a rock or a stump and sit around the campfire at night with two old soldiers who understood this warrior soul. We'll hear the wisdom of their soldierly experience—over eighty years of combined warrior experience in both special covert operations (asymmetrical warfare) and traditional "big army" force-on-force clashes (symmetrical warfare).

The conversation we're going to listen in on takes place just before these old warriors launch one final conclusive campaign together—a campaign, by the way, that's still impacting our world today, some 3,500 years later. Check tomorrow's newspaper; chances are good the Middle East will figure meaningfully on its pages.

In the next chapter we'll summarize the musings of these two old battle buddies into five critical ingredients of the warrior soul. Later we'll develop those principled ingredients more fully.

Don't doze off, soldier. This could save your life!

Chapter 3

GETTING A GRIP ON THE WARRIOR SOUL

A Matter of Spirit

The secret of victory lies not wholly in knowledge. It
lurks invisible in that vitalizing spark, intangible,
yet as evident as the lightning, the warrior soul.[1]
• GEN. GEORGE S. PATTON •

There is a soul to an army as well as to the individual
man, and no general can accomplish the full
work of his army unless he commands the soul
of his men, as well as their bodies and legs.[2]
• GEN. WILLIAM TECUMSEH SHERMAN •

IT WAS THERE at Lexington and Concord. It carried the day at
Little Round Top. It prevailed in the trenches of the Great War.
It stopped Hitler and Hirohito in their tracks. It was present in
spades at Pork Chop Hill and Heartbreak Ridge and the Chosin
Reservoir and in the hot red hillsides at Dak Pek and Lang Vei. It
ruled the desert for a hundred hours in Desert Storm. It held Task
Force Ranger together in a nightmare called Mogadishu. It still pre-
vails in our modern world in forsaken places like Ramadi, Mosul,

Tora Bora, and Kandahar. And it will carry the day in that war yet to come, the War to End All Wars.

It's the warrior soul.

What makes one man run to the guns while another runs away? Why does one man do the heroic while the next man cowers? What's the difference between a hero and a zero? It's that warrior soul. It's more than courage, deeper than bravery, stronger than "duty, honor, country." And in the critical moment it rules the man.

It's that intangible, internal spiritual force of character that carries a man in battle. The warrior soul is a majestic combination of mind, will, and emotion. Emerging from his spiritual core, it drives a man to sacrificial action.

Some appear to be born with it. Others develop it over time. But whether born or made, it stands out in all of life's battles.

All the great ones had it—George Washington. "Stonewall" Jackson. "Black Jack" Pershing. And Eisenhower, Abrams, Schwarzkopf, and Franks too.

Sam Whittemore had it, and so did thousands of other hometown boys unknown to us, citizen soldiers every one. The greatest of leaders are keenly aware that they owe their battlefield successes, their professional reputations, and their soldierly fame to every enlisted trooper in the rank and file who held his ground. Every GI worth his salt has carried some measure of the warrior soul in his chest, whether or not he understood it in those terms. In the crucible of combat it's that warrior soul beating in a thousand chests that has secured our nation's history. Far more potent than any advanced technology or weapons system, the warrior soul is the single greatest element in our national defense and security.

DNA OF THE WARRIOR SOUL

So just what is the warrior soul? It may be difficult to define, but you'll know it when you see it. It doesn't belong to a particular personality type. It's not necessarily bombastic and loud, but it is firm and resolute. It isn't flashy or charismatic, but it is rock-solid and immovable. Chiseled bodies hold no monopoly on it, but stout wills are at its core. It may not lead the cheers, but it does have a way of leading the thinking. It's not empty of fear, but it's full of courage. It may have doubts along the way, but it never, never, never quits.

The warrior soul is a matter of *spirit*. It resides in the intangible. It's a spiritual quality nurtured unseen in the internal fiber of a man's or woman's character. More spirit than sword. More heart than hand. More meditation than muscle. It's the warrior soul that most distinguishes a soldier on the battlefield.

Yes, every battle-worthy GI carries the warrior soul in his chest. And sometimes he carries a rope around his shoulder, as did one soldier whose name you've likely never heard.

Let me tell you about one such "dog" soldier whose story is known only to his family and a few friends. Though you may not have heard of Roy T. Graham, you celebrate his actions every year.

Roy Graham's ultimate boss was General Pershing. The two of them never met, but Pershing's reputation rested on the shoulders of men like Roy. Just one guy. A simple citizen soldier. As he would say, "Just doin' my part."

On one occasion Graham's part was swimming. Under fire. Across a river. With a rope around his shoulders.

Roy had grown up just a dirt-poor farm kid. But he raised his hand when his country called. The warrior soul breathed in Roy's chest. Like GIs everywhere, he was "impatient" with those who would rather stay behind at home and "protest" than do their warrior duty.

Among his letters home was a poem in his own handwriting, perhaps borrowed from *Songs in the Trenches*, but made his own and recorded in his soldier's pocket notebook. It was this young soldier's soulish call to courage:

SLACKER, you sit in your easy-chair,
Thanking the Lord you're not over there,
Where the cannons roar and the brave men die.

And, dying, perhaps unburied lie;
You may have purchased a bond or two
And imagine that is enough to do.

But some day, after the war is done
And victory by the brave is won,
You'll see men sneer as they pass you by,
And you'll wish you had not been afraid to die,
For what is the life of a coward worth
When he hasn't a friend on the lonely earth?

But the world may consent to forget some day,
And when it has done so, what will you say?[3]

Roy not only volunteered to serve in the army in the first place, but he also raised his hand a second time while he was a world away from his beloved fiancée. Like every successful warrior, Roy laid aside his personal comfort for the greater good of others—in this case, the nation. The warrior majors in sacrifice.

Take a stand. Join the struggle. Prepare to sacrifice. It's the DNA of the warrior soul.

Think about those words awhile in your own personal context. Where should *you* be "taking a stand, joining the struggle, and preparing to sacrifice"? Think through your world:

- Should you *stand*—take action—against the murder of children by abortion? Of course you should! Are you? How?

- How can you *join the struggle* with the local Christian bakery fined by the government because they hold marriage sacred and choose not to participate in a same-sex "marriage" ceremony by providing a cake? Show up. Figure out how to step alongside actively.

- How can you *sacrifice* in the battle? When was the last time you sent a significant donation to those leading the way for us believers—such as the Family Research Council in DC. Write some well-directed checks, warrior.

- Have you *joined the struggle* against terror by becoming personally informed regarding the nature of Islam and Islamic fundamentalism in particular? Can you intelligently address Sharia law and the threat posed to our faith and culture?

There are a thousand warrior causes out there for you—school boards, government encroachment in personal lives, persecution of Christians both here and abroad. There is no shortage of battles. Pick a couple and get in the fight.

One of the greatest spiritual warriors of the World War II generation was a young German by the name of Dietrich Bonhoeffer. He refused to bow to Hitler. He stood. He spoke up. He traveled to strengthen other Christians. And eventually it cost him his life. Just before he walked to the gallows, he told a friend, "This is the end, but for me the beginning." He'd fought well!

Bonhoeffer said something else that we need to take to heart every morning as we face the battles of our day: "Not to speak is to speak; not to act is to act."[4]

HEROIC MEN, HEROIC DEEDS

Let's get back to the trenches, literally. World War I wasn't going well. Our forces were bottled up, piling up casualties every day, and making no headway in closing with the Germans. The word had come down from "higher"—they had to cross that uncrossable river with significant mainline forces if they hoped to carry the day.

A trooper in Company B in the Engineer Battalion of the army's Second Division, Roy Graham raised his hand again. On a cold November day Roy and his fellow soldier and friend—his battle buddy—dove into the frigid waters of the Meuse River. Their orders were to establish an anchor point at the river's far side for what was to become a pontoon bridge.

With Roy carrying the rope, the two swimmers faced not only the current and the cold but heavy artillery and withering machine gun fire as well. They made the far bank and, working furiously, established the anchor point.

On the swim back across, Roy's partner was killed by enemy small arms fire. Roy pulled along his friend's body back to their unit.

The date was November 10, 1918. Later that same day Major General John A. Lejeune's Fifth Marines poured across the completed bridge and into the heart of the German lines, overwhelming the enemy.

The next day, November 11, the war was over. And to this day, every November 11, America slows her daily pace and thanks her veterans for her freedom.

By the way, I expect any marine reading these words can tell you who General Lejeune is. The marines rightly named one of their premier training facilities after that great soldier. After all, he did lead the charge that ended the Great War. His General Order on November 12, 1918, summed it up:

> On the night of November 10, heroic deeds were done by heroic men....In the last battle of the war, as in all others in which this division has participated, it enforced its will on the enemy.[5]

General Lejeune said it well enough. But he and his troops crossed that bridge on the shoulders of unnamed heroes like Roy T. Graham—simple men just doing their profound part. It's the warrior soul beating in the chests of both generals and corporals facing incredible obstacles that carries the day.

Let's restate the obvious. Those great marines, led by that great general, would never have had the opportunity to end that war were it not for a young "dogface" and his battle buddy who were willing to swim upstream against both current and bullets to pave the way.

You and I have never read of Roy in any books. Nor did Roy himself ever write one. But like GIs in every war, he did write letters home. Because I've had the privilege of knowing some of his descendants, I've read some of those letters. So far as I know, Roy's only account of those enormous actions of November 10, 1918, went like this: "If you want to read about some of the work we did, get a copy of the *Saturday Evening Post*....It talks about crossing the Meuse. This is where my friend from Salt Lake was killed."

That's it. Three sentences. Just a couple dozen words. All in a day's work for the warrior soul. No braggadocio. Just sacrifice. For Roy, it was all about the man next to him, his battle buddy. For us, it's all about "doin' your part" and being part of something much larger than yourself. So Christian warrior, pick your battle, grab a Christian battle buddy, and get in the fight. Take a stand. Join the struggle. Prepare to sacrifice. It's the DNA of the warrior soul.

By the way, Roy's example to his family still bears fruit. Part of his old uniform hangs on a wall in the family home of his granddaughter. And his great-grandson, a recent graduate of West Point, was serving in Iraq as these words were put to paper. This family *remembers*!

Roy T. Graham was one old soldier who never faded away. In chapters to come you'll learn more about the sheer power of a settled memory—the discipline of remembering—in weaving steel fiber into the warrior soul.

As far as I know, Roy never received a medal for his actions that day. But those actions were a great gift to the people of his country. Is it any wonder that every November 11 our nation celebrates the warrior soul in Roy, in General Lejeune, and in every veteran who has ever served in the armed forces of the United States of America? Way to go, Roy! From a small-town guy swimming a river under fire with a rope in his teeth, to a national holiday that honors every veteran and features the warrior soul.

We can take a lesson from Roy. How many times have you sacrificed and hardly anyone knows about it? Heaven knows! So begin to develop your sacrificial mind-set. Read. Read. Read. Have you ever identified with some of the spiritual warriors who have gone before you? Do you read biographies? Have you given a season of more intense study to some of the great warriors in faith's hall of fame? Start with those named in Hebrews 11. Developing a "settled memory" of those principled warriors who have gone ahead of you is very much a part of developing your own warrior soul. We'll talk more about that in a chapter to come.

READY WARRIORS

The greatest warrior soul is the one that thrived in the chest of the greatest warrior ever. Jesus Christ is His name. The Bible portrays Him straight up as one incredible warrior. Let's look again at that description in Revelation 19:

> In righteousness He judges and wages war. His eyes are a flame of fire.... From His mouth comes a sharp sword, so that with it He may strike down the nations, and He will rule them with a rod of iron; and He treads the wine press of the fierce wrath of God, the Almighty.
>
> —REVELATION 19:11–12, 15

Many great figures in Scripture shared that warrior soul. There are numerous ancient biblical examples of it, written at a time when warfare was much different, much more in-your-face. These were days when men not only went to war but also often journeyed to the battlefield with their whole families in tow.

The father of our biblical faith, Abraham, had a warrior soul. A coalition of outlaw tribes had raided the Valley of Siddim, robbed the residents of everything including goods and food, and moved north in their escape. In the process they carried off some of the local residents as slaves. One of those captives was Abraham's nephew. Bad choice on the bad guys' part! That put Abraham—known then as Abram—in the fight. Consider this personal translation of Genesis 14:14–16:

> And when Abram heard that a member of his family had been taken captive, he saddled up [the actual word means "mustered," a military term] three hundred and eighteen of his well-trained men and went in pursuit.... He divided his forces by night against the enemy, he and his men, and defeated them...and he brought back all the goods, his nephew, and all the other captured people.

Maybe a banner hung over Abraham's tent that read, "Don't tread on me." But in any case he took action—plenty of it—and I'm sure when the battle was over, the enemy was sorry they'd tangled with this warrior-at-the-ready. Abraham and his men traveled on foot over scores of miles, conducted a difficult night operation without modern means of communication, and decisively won the battle.

At the conclusion of this operation, the victory was celebrated with a sacred meal of worship and thanksgiving to "God Most High," who had delivered Abraham's enemies into his hands (Gen. 14:18–20.) Abraham, in an extraordinary act of humble worship, refused any share of the "loot," choosing not to profit personally from his skill as a warrior. Sounds like our kind of man.

Abraham was merely one of a long list of God-honoring warriors in Scripture. Moses also carried the warrior soul in his chest. He demonstrated it on numerous battlefields and wrote of it in the war memorial poem that we find in Exodus 15:

I will sing to the LORD, for He is highly exalted;
The horse and its rider He has hurled into the sea....
The LORD is a warrior; The LORD is His name....
Your right hand, O LORD, is majestic in power,
Your right hand, O LORD, shatters the enemy.

—EXODUS 15:1, 3, 6

Following Moses, the man Joshua also demonstrated the warrior soul in a soldier's career stretching across more than four decades.

Centuries later David evidenced the warrior soul from his boyhood. In one of his great psalms he would write this about the Lord he loved: "Bless the LORD, who is my rock. He gives me strength for war and skill for battle."[6] In another psalm David (remembering the spiritual and physical exhilaration of combat) gives this shout to God: "By You I can run upon a troop; and by my God I can leap over a wall" (Ps. 18:29).

Many other biblical heroes were also soldiers in whose chests beat the warrior heart, the warrior soul. Read, for example, the first sergeant's morning report in 1 Chronicles 11. The Holy Spirit here honors the dirt soldier, the dogface, by listing name after name on the unit roster.

Again, the critical point is this: it's the warrior soul in every soldier that carries the day—not muscle, not firepower, not technology, not weaponry. What carries the day is what carries the warrior: his soul. It's what a man believes down deep in his heart that makes him a warrior.

Notice that all of the men we've mentioned in this chapter were biblical believers. They served their God as well as their families and people. We'll come back to that; it bears a closer look. War, at its center, is always a spiritual matter. The physicality is overwhelming, but the center of the conflict is always spiritual in one form or another. It's the spiritual fitness of the heart that's ultimately the most critical element to the warrior.

The US Army recognizes this reality. In an intentional effort to build the warrior soul, the army has launched a program titled Comprehensive Soldier Fitness: Strong Minds, Strong Bodies. The program's director, Brigadier General Rhonda Cornum, explains that "Being *Army Strong* is, in fact, being more than just physically fit."[7] The official description of the campaign amplifies that reality:

> It is mental and emotional strength. It is the confidence to lead. It is the courage to stand up for your beliefs. It is the compassion to help others. It is the desire for lifelong learning. It is the intelligence to make the right decision. It is making a difference for yourself, your family, your community, and our nation.[8]

This commitment to spiritual fitness is meant "to build the resilience and enhance the performance of every Soldier," as well as every member of that soldier's family; it envisions "an Army of balanced, healthy, self-confident Soldiers…whose resilience and total fitness enables them to thrive in an era of high operational tempo and persistent conflict."[9]

And you have to respect the army's particular definition of *resilience*: "the ability to grow and thrive in the face of challenges and bounce back from adversity."[10] Indeed.

War has a way of stretching the soul, of pressuring the soldier's internal compass and forcing him to make critical choices in the way he sees himself, others, and life itself. Facing life-or-death ultimates has a way of sifting, straining, and sorting out our deepest values, our core beliefs. *What's worth dying for? What's worth living for?* Ultimate questions like that are best dealt with in our ultimate field manual; the warrior soul is best shaped by an intimate familiarity with God and His Word. It makes sense then—doesn't it?— that we search the Scriptures to identify the most critical elements of the warrior soul. It shouldn't surprise us that the Bible would teach us about this critical core.

One of America's premier warriors may have said it best. General

George C. Marshall—the army chief of staff during World War II, the man who placed Eisenhower in his central role, the man who as America's secretary of state so skillfully rebuilt Europe after the war—put it this way:

> The soldier's heart, the soldier's spirit, the soldier's soul, are everything. Unless the soldier's soul sustains him he cannot be relied on and will fail himself and his commander and his country in the end.[11]

INTRODUCING THE DOG

In this book we're going to take a closer look at one of those biblical heroes in whose chest the warrior's heart beat with an irrepressible rhythm. He was Joshua's battle buddy. His name personifies the warrior soul in five little letters—Caleb was his name; battle was his game.

His name in some ancient Near Eastern languages is translated simply "Dog." It was a moniker intended to reflect "loyalty and faithfulness to his master." Appropriately enough, the God of Scripture speaks of him as "My servant Caleb" (Num. 14:24), a title of highest honor that God had previously reserved only for the greatest of leaders, Moses himself. Caleb was a legend in his own time, and today we're still naming our children after him.

Caleb was a "dog" soldier who was rigorous enough to be running long-range recon at age forty and still eager for battle in his eighties, much like old Sam Whittemore. Caleb was an old soldier who never surrendered.

We'll draw our character sketch of this warrior from a 3,500-year-old after-action report. It's all recorded in God's Word in Joshua 14. This very special historical narrative, to be read and interpreted differently than a New Testament doctrinal epistle, is wonderfully revealing. This ancient report allows us to distinguish at least five key principles that bear heavily on the shaping of the warrior soul. Let them take root in your own soul.

Chapter 4

FIVE CORE REALITIES

Shaping Every Soldier for Life and Its Battles

What, then, is the soul of battle? A rare thing
indeed that arises only when free men march
unabashedly toward the heartland of their
enemy in hopes of saving the doomed, when
their vast armies are aimed at salvation and
liberation, not conquest and enslavement. Only
then does battle take on a spiritual dimension.[1]
• VICTOR DAVIS HANSON •

WAR IN THE fifteenth century BC was largely *mano y mano*.
Shields, bucklers, and swords clashed, powered by biceps, tri-
ceps, and deltoids. Human muscle. In such a combat environment the giants among men naturally tended to have a certain
resilience. It was a dog-eat-dog, survival-of-the-fittest culture.

And the biggest dogs were usually the biggest winners. In such
a world, for a man to be battle-fit for more than a few years took
some doing. Military "careers" tended to be, on the simple face of
it, short-lived more often than not.

Enter Caleb.

Enter spiritual power.

Enter moral purpose.

Enter the warrior soul.

WARRIOR WISDOM

Caleb was an iron man before there was an Iron Age. Caleb was the Cal Ripken of the ancient Israeli Defense Force. The man caught hold of an abiding principle: a soldier's muscle power is less critical than his spiritual power. It's the heart and soul of the warrior that ultimately carries the day.

Caleb, one of the Old Testament's great warriors, is a treasure trove of 3,500-year-old wisdom that has stood the test of time.

As the Israeli slaves managed to escape Egypt, cross through the deadly waters of the Red Sea, crawl their way through wilderness, and eventually move toward their promising future in Canaan as a new nation, it was the men who led the way, one special group of men in particular—twelve warriors who ran the long-range recon patrols. They were the tip of the spear.

Two of these special ops soldiers set themselves apart by demonstrating, in the words of Scripture, hearts that were especially "strong and courageous" (Josh. 1:6–7).

Each of the twelve men selected for this earliest recorded Special Forces A-Team was noted for his leadership, his well-honed military skills, and his ability to thrive behind enemy lines. The twelve tribes of Israel ran their "selection and assessment" process, and the "best ranger" from each tribe was carefully chosen for this particularly dangerous operation. They were such outstanding individuals that Scripture gives them the special recognition of listing their names in an exceptional unit roster in the thirteenth chapter of the Book of Numbers.

The best of these twelve, a member of the tribe of Ephraim, was appointed the team leader. His name was Hoshea, the son of Nun. Moses called him Joshua, the name we remember him by. His well-earned fame has extended over thirty-five centuries so far.

Joshua's more-than-competent assistant team leader was Caleb. Given the soul that beat in the chests of these two warriors, it's not surprising we're still naming our sons after both of them.

Their mission, essentially the same for all reconnaissance teams in every age, was to scout out the land—to evaluate its characteristics, appraise its strategic value, measure its military strength, and particularly describe its fortifications. They were to bring back actionable intelligence regarding the land's occupants, the Canaanites.

The mission lasted for weeks. As it turned out, ten members of that original team lost their nerve somewhere between their departure and their return to friendly lines. Seeing with their own eyes the sheer numbers and size of indigenous defense forces and the number and type of fortified cities, these ten panicked, backed down, and reported that their nation's goal of taking over that land was impossible.

It was as though they had gone on CNN before a national audience, wide-eyed and filled with fear over what they'd seen as eyewitnesses. Worse yet, their report struck fear into the hearts of the entire nation.

However, two of the twelve—Joshua and Caleb—were seeing with different eyes, and they delivered quite a different report.

These two team leaders knew each other especially well, having been "ranger buddies" for years, both militarily and spiritually. The two of them viewed reality with similar eyes, fed each other's perspective and courage, and were intensely loyal to each other and to God. (If only Moses had sent just the two of them—how different the history of that nation would have unfolded!) It was the kind of mutual support they greatly needed when their fellow team members fell prey to cowardice. Caleb and Joshua stood their ground and encouraged the people to launch the invasion of Canaan immediately. What the ten lacked, the two owned in spades.

To borrow the words of today's US Army, Joshua and Caleb were "resilient" warriors who possessed the "ability to grow and thrive in the face of challenges."[2] They possessed—again in the words of our modern Comprehensive Soldier Fitness program—a "set of beliefs, principles, or values that sustain a person beyond family, institutional, and societal sources of strength."[3]

To say that another way, Joshua and Caleb were characterized by spiritual fortitude.

What exactly were their beliefs? Their principles? Their values? How did these things "sustain" them? How do they sustain anyone with a strength that's "beyond" our normal sources of strength such as family and friends and others?

These two men possessed a way of viewing reality beyond the obvious horizontal perspectives on the part of more "average" soldiers. These men were way above average. They weren't "also-rans." They weren't just a couple more military bodies. These guys possessed some keen sense of reality; they "saw" things that lesser men missed entirely.

How so? How did they "see"? What kind of "eyes" did they have? Some kind of paranormal x-ray vision? Well…yes, sort of. But it isn't necessarily exceptional. It's the kind of vision available to *every* human being—*if* they'll choose to apply it to real life.

Call it "the eyes of the heart."

I believe Joshua and Caleb possessed what Paul, the great New Testament apostle, referred to when he prayed for the Ephesians and believers everywhere: "that *the eyes of your heart* may be enlightened, so that you will know what is the hope of His calling, what are the riches of the glory of His inheritance in the saints, and what is the surpassing greatness of His power toward us who believe" (Eph. 1:18–19).

Caleb's eyes were keenly developed in sync with his soul. Caleb "saw" beyond the horizontal norm.

ALWAYS SAFE

Other warriors have demonstrated similar qualities—Stonewall Jackson, for instance.

Like Caleb, Stonewall Jackson saw reality with the spiritual eyes of the heart. On one occasion during the Civil War Jackson demonstrated a quality that simply stunned others around him. The scene was remarkable. General Jackson had just received a dispatch from a fellow officer elsewhere on the battlefield. Action was hot and heavy, with artillery raining down "danger close."

As Jackson was reading the fresh dispatch, an exploding cannonball disintegrated a tree beside him and rained bark, wood, and other debris on Jackson and those nearby, including the dispatch. Simply brushing the debris aside, Jackson continued to read, entirely unruffled, and clearly with no sense of alarm at any immediate threats. One of his men standing there asked him how on earth he could maintain his composure surrounded by such traumatic chaos, stress, and mortal threat. Jackson—a believer in the same God whom Caleb followed—responded, "My religious belief teaches me to feel as safe in battle as in bed."[4]

Jackson's deep-rooted personal faith in the clear statements of the God of the Bible rendered him completely confident in the most dire circumstances. Like Caleb before him, Jackson believed the God of the Bible to be so supremely sovereign over everything from snowflakes to bombshells that God's followers—Jackson among them—were in fact invincible and immortal until God chose to bring them "home." In that spirit Jackson uttered his final words before dying after the battle at Chancellorsville: "Let us cross over the river and rest under the shade of the trees"[5]—the "rest" of God's eternal kingdom.

Unfortunately for the people of Israel thirty-five centuries ago, Joshua and Caleb were a minority—as is typically true for true leaders of vision in most societies. True leadership is usually a lonesome calling. Because Joshua and Caleb's fellow soldiers, as well as the population at large, refused to follow their foresight in their minority report, the nation consequently struggled in insecurity for the next forty years.

Nevertheless, Caleb—always faithful and ever ready—soldiered well in the ensuing years of Israel's south-to-north conquest of the land, a campaign summarized in chapter 12 of the Book of Joshua. Joshua 13 tells us, however, that the toughest portions of the land remained unconquered. The Israelite army had broken the enemy's main opposition, but the toughest objectives remained undefeated.

As an aside here, let me note that the reason for their failure to conquer all the land was their reluctance to sacrifice sufficiently. Like the populations of most nations, including our own, the general Israeli populace just wanted "peace"—as cheaply as possible, as soon as possible. False peace. They didn't bother to look deeply into the issues to discern the long-term dangers. Left to themselves, most people will choose temporary personal comfort over long-term principles. How about you, soldier? See to it that this does not describe you. Choose the long-term "difficult" over the immediate "easy."

Most Israelis in Caleb's day were willing to settle for short-term "peace" but failed to foresee the inevitable consequences of ignoring the determined values of their enemy. They stopped short. Sound familiar? Do you see any parallels with America's current reluctance to recognize Islam for what it is—so much more than a religion, but a totalitarian system of governance to include absolute control over the financial, economic, political, social, and spiritual aspects of human life? But we digress here.

As a warrior, Caleb was out of step among a people who—for the sake of peace, comfort, and wealth—had no taste for warfare.

Telling Phrases

Back to Joshua 13. With the main-force opposition broken, only the toughest enemy strongholds remained. By the time we come to Joshua 14, the land is largely in Israel's control. Only the most challenging and unconquerable portions remain. This last and most difficult part of the campaign is the background for Caleb's encounter with Joshua in Joshua 14:6–15.

I picture the two old warriors sitting around a campfire on the night before they and their troops cross the line of departure for this final mission. Their conversation is a treasure of wisdom for the heart of every warrior.

In the words Caleb speaks here, several important phrases stand out, each revealing an essential quality of the warrior soul. Take the old warrior's pulse as you listen to him briefing his battle buddy, Joshua, just before they once more launch an offensive—together. Take special note of the phrases I've highlighted, and consider what they reveal about the warrior soul.

> Then the sons of Judah drew near to Joshua in Gilgal, and Caleb the son of Jephunneh the Kenizzite said to him, "*You know the word which the Lord spoke* to Moses the man of God concerning *you and me* in Kadesh-barnea. I was forty years old when Moses the servant of the LORD sent me from Kadesh-barnea to spy out the land, and I brought word back to him *as it was in my heart.*
>
> "Nevertheless my brethren who went up with me made the heart of the people melt with fear; but *I followed the Lord my God fully....*
>
> "Now behold, the LORD has let me live, just as He spoke, these forty-five years, from the time that the LORD spoke this word to Moses, when Israel walked in the wilderness; and now behold, I am eighty-five years old today. I am still as strong today as I was in the day Moses sent me; as my strength was then, so my strength is now, for war and for going out and coming in.
>
> "Now then, give me this hill country about which the LORD spoke on that day, for you heard on that day that Anakim were there, with great fortified cities; *perhaps the LORD will be with me, and I will drive them out* as the LORD has spoken."
>
> —JOSHUA 14:6–12

I believe those highlighted phrases give us insight into keys that will sustain every one of us in the battles of this life. Each phrase reveals a key element of the magnificent warrior soul that was beating in Caleb's chest:

"You know the word which the Lord spoke...

Here Caleb draws upon some history; he relates the current situation to its historical roots, bringing the past to bear upon the present. Caleb sees the current realities through the lens of studied history, an invaluable warrior skill. Ultimately this points us to the full Word of God. This phrase in the text can also be rendered, *"Remember what the LORD said"* (Josh. 14:6, NLT)—a deliberate recalling.

"You and me..."

Just three little words—and we often spout those same words too casually. But there's nothing casual here for Caleb; he and Joshua know each other; there's a track record of loyalty to each other, of facing enormous difficulties together. There's a world of reality and commitment behind those words. "You and me, Joshua" reflects a lifetime of battlefield faithfulness and camaraderie. These two old soldiers have had each other's backs for decades now. Once more they step out—together. They experienced the battlefield camaraderie among soldiers that defies definition.

"As it was in my heart...

Caleb indicates his choice to see more than the merely physical. He's motivated by vision beyond the visible. The eyes of his heart provide his governing insights; these spiritual eyes lift his gaze from the obvious physical realities to a level of spiritual understanding of the larger picture. Caleb believes something beyond the obvious and merely physical. The bigger picture is spiritual, moral, just, and principled. More specifically, it's rooted in an abiding principle that passes the test of time and is true in every day and age. It is utterly transcendent. And it drives Caleb's warrior soul.

"I followed the LORD my God fully."

The verb here, in the original language, is an unusually powerful little compound: "followed fully." Caleb indicates there is a kind of "following" that's more than merely coming along behind. *Following fully* (Moses used the same comprehensive word in describing Caleb in Joshua 14:9) indicates a qualitative kind of following that bears an incredibly focused personal intensity, a following of spiritual guidance that's way beyond the casual. Caleb's commitment to God, to God's Word, and to God's principles is *total*. He is a fully devoted follower of the God of heaven and earth—the same God, by the way, to whom our Founding Fathers appealed in our nation's Declaration of Independence.

"Perhaps the LORD will be with me, and I will drive them out."

Here Caleb's words reflect two great biblical principles—God's full sovereignty and our human responsibility. There's no smugness here. Caleb knows there are no guarantees in this life; it's possible he won't succeed. The old warrior may be killed on this mission. But he also recognizes that his mission and indeed his very life are in God's hands. With this humble but disciplined biblical confidence Caleb is prepared to do his duty. He will launch the mission, give it all he's got, and trust God for His intended results. Caleb's optimism is unflagging.

These ancient words represent, for me, the timeless qualities of the warrior soul. Taken together, they provide for the sustaining of our souls through all of life's battles, whether physical, spiritual, or both. Let's take a stab at identifying those qualities.

THE WARRIOR SOUL:
FIVE KEY ELEMENTS

Pondering further Caleb's words, we can explore five key elements that shape the soldier for life's battles.

1. A sense of transcendent cause

Caleb sees and grasps the big picture—the "why we fight." He can do this so well because he has a grasp of the grand scheme, the view from thirty thousand feet. Caleb is joined to something much larger than himself, and he knows it. The old warrior is alert to the grand scheme, to the big picture, to what the Bible reveals as God's kingdom program. He views more than the fields of fire in front of him; he sees the current circumstances in the context of larger realities.

Caleb comprehends God's larger kingdom program as well as his own part in it. This isn't just one more battle in thousands of years of dustups. This is part and parcel of a holy God's strategy for His chosen people. In other words, Caleb sees with spiritual foresight—with the eyes of his heart, or as Caleb expresses it (in Joshua 14:7), "as it was in my heart."

2. A settled memory

Caleb reviews and grasps history so that he has an "anchor" in his soul. Caleb sees the linkage between history and his current circumstances. In this case, it is spiritually divine history, God's very Word(s). The Bible is just that. As the old poem teaches, though through the ages skeptic blows have beat upon it, the Bible, like the blacksmith's anvil, wears out the hammers.[6] History's floor is littered with the shattered hammers of biblical critics. (I recall starting seminary with the nagging fear that I—what youthful arrogance!—would be the poor sap who discovered some tiny error in the prophet Jeremiah and the whole house of cards would come tumbling down. I have to chuckle today, but it was a very real, fearful doubt at the time.)

At eighty-five Caleb has grown well beyond the doubts common to all of us in our younger, and lesser, days. He knows the truth expressed later in Kierkegaard's famous observation: "Life can only be understood backwards; but it must be lived forwards."[7] Caleb got that. He's keenly aware that he stands on what others

have achieved, gained, ascertained in the past. He places the immediate campaign in its historical context. It's an awareness that surfaces in the habitual phrases Caleb uses throughout this passage:
"remember what the LORD said"; "on that day"; "just as He spoke";
"the LORD spoke this word"; "the LORD spoke on that day"; "as the
LORD has spoken."

True faith is always digging into the past. *Nurtured memories
shape present realities and determine future destinies.* (Spend some
time thinking that last sentence over.) This present campaign is
part of something much larger than it might first appear, and the
lessons of the past provide exactly what the soldier needs to prevail
in the present.

Every current campaign involves the past.

Let me say that again—*every current conflict involves the past.*
History is incredibly relevant! And it is even more intensely relevant when people refuse to recognize it. If we forget the past, we
lose perspective for the present as well as direction for the future.
Caleb knew that. Life in his eighties had everything to do with life
in his forties, and he was determined not to forget. Things like old
documents, or a treasured letter, or a story or testimony of another
soldier, or family lore—in Caleb's case, covenants and promises,
nothing less than God's Word itself—bear directly on the soldier's
present situation. The current challenges bring the previous decades
to climax.

It's true in the big picture, such as the invasion of Canaan. And
it's true in Caleb's own personal picture because he took it to heart.
For Caleb, time—past or present—was never wasted. Christian soldier, do you see your own personal historic timeline as a thread
connecting you to the grace and purposes of God you enjoy today?

Caleb recognized he was standing on the shoulders of those
who'd gone before him. He knew he held a precious baton passed
to him from his past—personal, national, and spiritual. Will he
drop it, or will he carry it successfully? How about you? Do you see

yourself in something of a spiritually potent relay race for the generations yet to be born? (See Psalm 78:6.)

Caleb views this challenging battle ahead, this coming "dark hour" of combat (what Teddy Roosevelt would call his "crowded hour"), as the heaviest of responsibilities and the greatest of opportunities for his family, his country, and the generations to come. Caleb has a "settled memory," and he draws power for the present from the principles of the past, knowing full well the future, and its generations, will profit from it.

3. A personal intensity

Caleb is wired. His sense of transcendent cause and his settled memory allow him to greet the current challenge with great personal intensity. He's motivated by all the right things. As a result, he's *eager* for the challenges, *undistracted* by personal issues, and stays *intensely focused* on their *mission first*—so much so that he volunteers, once again, to be in the center of the battle at its hottest point.

He volunteers for the most difficult terrain and objective—the hill country, which is occupied by the Anakim. The sons of Anak were the notorious "giants" who, forty years earlier, had struck such immobilizing fear in the hearts of the ten and of the nation. Caleb is determined to close the chapter on fear and defeat.

Caleb's intensity is demonstrated in his capacity to "follow fully" the Lord. It's the fickle who fail to follow.

4. An unflagging optimism

Caleb exudes a soldier's proper confidence, however difficult the assignment may be. Don't mistake this for mere bravado. This is a soldier's measured confidence that the cause is right and worthy, and the hour is at hand. It's time to pull the trigger.

Theologians might call it a confident trust in the hand of Providence. Others might call it a warrior's determination to fulfill his duty no matter what. Call it what you will, it's an absolute commitment to "never surrender."

Caleb's unflagging optimism is seen in his closing phrase: "Perhaps the LORD will be with me, and I shall drive them out as the LORD has spoken." This "perhaps" is not the voice of doubt so much as the voice of experience and expectancy. As a soldier Caleb knows there's no guarantee, but as a believer he also knows the God who holds his life in His hands. He's seen it many times along his life's path. Here Caleb rightly recognizes the freedom of his sovereign God. He also knows His promised presence with him even if he should face the shadow of death.

How many times in our own lives do we come to the point where we must say, "Well, I've done all I know how to do. It's really out of my hands now. God will have to see to it. The results are in His hands."

Is that not what another great spiritual warrior named Abraham experienced? Think through Genesis 22 and imagine the father and son walking up the hill of sacrifice together. On the way up what must have seemed like a very long hike to Abraham, Isaac asked his father, "I see the fire and wood, but no lamb?" True enough. And it didn't really add up for Abraham either—"God promised me a son; now He directs me to kill him?"

Abraham didn't know how all this was supposed to come together. But Abraham's answer to Isaac is a lesson in faith and trust for every spiritual warrior. In the final analysis it is our faith in God and our trust in His ways that produce in us an unflagging optimism. Abraham was determined to do his part and leave the outcome to God. When he said to Isaac, "God will provide," he did not yet know the end of the story himself. What he said to Isaac was essentially, "I don't get it either, son. God is going to have to see to this Himself."

So it was similarly with Caleb. And with Bonhoeffer—what looked like the end of his life was merely the beginning of real life, eternally. I like to call it unflagging optimism. Have you developed a good reservoir of it in your own life?

Caleb is confident but not cocky. His confidence is both humble and disciplined. His words exude unshakable trust in the Lord he knows personally. So it should be with us.

5. A deep camaraderie

Caleb knows by experience the value of a deep personal commitment to his fellow warriors. Our text in Joshua 14 doesn't so much emphasize this in written words, but the spirit of it permeates this conversation. The very fact that Joshua and Caleb are having such a consequential discussion demonstrates their commitment to each other.

You can hear it as well in Caleb's reminder to Joshua in verse 6: "You know the word which the LORD spoke...*concerning you and me.*" There's a lifetime of soldiering together in those words, a deep mutual sense of loyalty and trust that needs few words. In fact, it reaches much deeper than words. It's a loyalty known only to men who've faced together the horrors of combat. There's a deep sense of brotherhood among men who've tasted battle, who've "seen the elephant" of combat, who've faced the incredible nightmare of armed adversity...and survived.

And so it is with Christian warriors. How often have I sat at breakfast in the morning with a couple of my spiritual battle buddies and we've worked through the challenges in our lives. We know the pressures in one another's marriages. We know the stressors in one another's businesses. We know the pains of our parenting. And we strengthen one another in those struggles. Then, from time to time, we sit around the fire or on the back deck—as we did just last evening—and rehearse battles past and the goodness and faithfulness of our God in them. We walk away strengthened for the next day's battles. We walk away knowing we are not going into those battles alone. We have fellow reliable warriors at our side.

A transcendent cause....settled memory....personal intensity...an unflagging optimism....deep camaraderie—five realities, five core aspects of the essence of the warrior soul. They're calling out to us, awaiting our exploration. And that's our mission in these next five chapters. Hang on, soldier.

Chapter 5

A TRANSCENDENT CAUSE

The Engine That Drives the Warrior Soul

They had no right to win. Yet they did, and in doing
so they changed the course of a war....Even against
the greatest of odds, there is something in the human
spirit—a magic blend of skill, faith and valor—that
can lift men from certain defeat to incredible victory.[1]
• WALTER LORD, ON THE BATTLE OF MIDWAY •

TWO OF MY sons have run and completed marathons, one in Chicago and one in Portland. Personally I'm not much enamored with that kind of running—unless, of course, one's life depended on it. For my part, I've always teased my "runner" friends, insisting there's really no such thing as a "fun run."

The marathon makes my point.

Essentially it's twenty-six miles of sheer "keeping on keeping on." Every marathoner knows of the feared "hitting the wall," when it seems there's nothing left, no strength, no oxygen, no muscle, no desire...no forward progress...no nothing! Just an out-of-body collapse.

What is it that drives a runner to somehow run right on through that wall and keep moving ahead to finish the course? Most such runners will tell you it's something down inside, deep down. It's a "will."

Such a will, I submit, is part of the soul. Simply put, our souls are a spiritual combination of our minds, our emotions, and our wills.

In fact, many marathoners describe such running as a genuinely spiritual experience. I believe they're onto something. The demands of a marathon take you beyond your normal capacity, beyond the physical—even, dare we say, beyond yourself. It takes you where, left to yourself, you don't normally go. Yes, it truly can be a kind of spiritual experience.

That experience, as all significant spiritual experiences usually do, begins with a choice: the decision to run. The experience takes on a life of its own and "grows" you through the training period. It reaches the peak in the race itself, particularly when the finish line is in sight.

Let's try to trace that process through the soul. The mind thinks. With time those thoughts settle (call it ruminating, even meditating). And when those thoughts get to the point of settling about eighteen inches below the brain—somewhere deep in the chest—then those thoughts begin to gel into something called character.

That character, like a muscle under ongoing pressure and exercise, continues to expand to the point that it firms up and hardens into a matter of will. And that will, forged in the crucible, becomes the reservoir out of which the myriad of life's decisions are made, especially the larger choices—including the will to keep on keeping on. Let's ruminate some here right now—and every morning. Let's think through the battles to come.

A Three-Part Process

A look inward

One long-distance runner, an acquaintance I respect greatly, said that his training for these events started every day with a "look inward"—the self-assessment that's fundamental to every warrior. My friend always readied himself by taking something of a personal inventory, raising his eyes upward toward heaven, and seeking to encourage his own soul by telling himself, "You can make it today."[2]

That's essentially what David, the great warrior-king, was doing when he composed many of his psalms; he took inventory, then directed his weaknesses toward God's supply. Under the inspiration of the Spirit he spoke to his own soul.

For example, in two adjacent psalms David calls out three times, "Why are you cast down, O my soul, and why are you in turmoil within me?" Preaching to himself each time, David repeatedly comes back to this affirmation: "Hope in God; for I shall again praise him, my salvation and my God" (Ps. 42:5–6, 11; 43:5, ESV).

A look upward

David shows us that our training continues with another look. This second one is a "look upward"—a tuning of the soul to the things of the spirit.

As a warrior, David's life was continually under serious threat. Like any reasonable man, he knew he would need more strength in the face of the enemy than he could routinely manufacture in his own ability. He therefore practiced—with prayer—this second training element. His faith in God had a central role in the challenges he was to face. And inevitably that inner reflection before God produced the kind of confidence essential to mission effectiveness.

In many moments, in many tight straits, David prayed thoughts and wrote words inspired by the Spirit of God, like these words recorded in what we might call his soldier's journal:

> I will lift up my eyes to the mountains; from where shall my help come? My help comes from the LORD, who made heaven and earth.... He who keeps you will not slumber.... The LORD is your keeper.... The LORD will guard your going out and your coming in from this time forth and forever.
>
> —PSALM 121

To You I lift up my eyes, O You who are enthroned in the heavens!...As the eyes of servants look to the hand of their master...so our eyes look to the LORD our God.

—PSALM 123:1–2

The king is not saved by a mighty army; a warrior is not delivered by great strength. A horse is a false hope for victory; nor does it deliver anyone by its great strength. Behold, the eye of the LORD is on those who fear Him....Our soul waits for the LORD; He is our help and our shield.

—PSALM 33:16–20

I wait quietly before God, for my victory comes from him. He alone is my rock and my salvation, my fortress where I will never be shaken....Let all that I am wait quietly before God, for my hope is in him....My victory and honor come from God alone. He is my refuge, a rock where no enemy can reach me.

—PSALM 62:1–7, NLT

A look outward

Having looked inward in self-inventory and needs assessment, and then upward in focusing on the living God as a resource, David was free to "look outward" at the course to be run. He was able to visualize the objectives, the obstacles, the routes, and the necessary strategies to complete the course ahead.

This same three-part process is essentially what Joshua and Caleb, to whom we'll return shortly, were doing around the campfire that night before they launched the mission to take the notorious hill country around ancient Hebron.

Since war, in the final analysis, is ultimately a spiritual exercise, warriors stepping onto the battlefield are confronted with ultimates like fear, inner loneliness, outward terror, even overwhelmingly shocking rage—and death. This horrific trauma and confusion and chaos of combat has pushed men in every war, in every century, to reach outside themselves for the spiritual realities. No one has said it more transparently than Lieutenant General A. A. Vandegrift, the man who commanded the First Marine Division to victory at Guadalcanal:

> I do sincerely believe one thing; every man on Guadalcanal came to sense a "Power" above himself. There was a reality there greater than any human force. It is literally true—there are no atheists in foxholes—religion is precious under fire.[3]

Our current global war with the Islamo-fascists is no different. The battlefields of Afghanistan and Iraq pushed men to personal spiritual evaluation. The reports—on the nightly news, in articles from imbedded reporters, and in soldiers' personal correspondence—are commonplace. They tell of Bible studies, prayer meetings, baptisms, and well-attended worship services. All this represents a reality that author Stephen Mansfield has succinctly observed:

> War forces a definition of belief. It strips away the superficial and even the cultural and leaves only what is relevant in the face of death, horror, and fear. War filters, refines, and distills. It presses against faith with a driving practicality, with a demand for real-world meaning.[4]

The man-centered philosophical rubbish flowing from too many college lecterns out of the mouths of untested and self-satisfied "intellectuals" has a way of evaporating at the first sound of an incoming round. It's this way in all wars.

As it did with me, war drove Winston Churchill to abandon his intellectualized and fashionable atheism and to return, with a new and very personal zeal, to the faith of his fathers. Churchill recorded his personal revival, pounded out on the anvil of combat and the pressures of a POW camp, in his own words in *My Early Life,* first published in 1930:

I found no comfort in any of the philosophical ideas which some men parade in their hours of ease and strength and safety. They seemed only fair-weather friends. I realized with awful force that no exercise of my own feeble wit and strength could save me from my enemies, and that without the assistance of that High Power which interferes in the eternal sequence of cause and effects more often than we are always prone to admit, I could never succeed. I prayed long and earnestly for help and guidance. My prayer, as it seems to me, was swiftly and wonderfully answered.[5]

Learning a Heritage

To this day the scene tingles in my heart. I grew up in a small coal-mining community. Our family lived on Third Street (there were only three). Near the end of our street stood the "city hall"—in reality just a glorified garage for the volunteer firemen's only fire truck. Just out front near the sidewalk stood a small, black-slate wall flanked by two giant World War II artillery pieces. Etched in the slate were the names of those men who had left our tiny town to serve in the US military during that war. All gave some; some gave all.

The names of my dad and his brothers were there, along with scores of other names I recognized from the mailboxes in front of the modest homes lining our three streets. Every name was meaningful to me.

The names that awed me most on that wall were the ones listed "above the line." Across the top of the memorial ran a line to set apart the names of the men who never returned. They had given all…everything…the last full measure—their very lives.

Dad told me they had given their lives so we could be free—to worship as we wished, to think and say whatever we wished, and to walk down Third Street whenever we wanted. We were free because of the sacrifice of these men.

I was in awe. I still am. I can feel the sensation in my chest and eyes at this moment.

One name in particular stood out to me. He'd been Dad's friend, a high school buddy. They swam in the river together and marched to the same tune. In fact, Doug Munro was the drum major while Dad was the bass drummer in our town's little drum and bugle corps. Doug had enlisted early, asked Dad to take his girl to the prom, and reported for duty.

On September 27, 1942, Doug gave his all. He died at a place called Guadalcanal while rescuing a battalion of marines trapped on a beach and being slaughtered.

On the hill above "city hall" was our town's small cemetery. Occasionally we would visit Doug's grave, and I would stand in awe. Doug's grave bore the emblem of our nation's highest award for valor in combat, the Medal of Honor.

At first my awe was the simple hero worship of a small boy for a big man. As the years passed and I thought more about the reality of it all, I asked Dad why a guy would do what Doug did—volunteer to run straight into the teeth of the guns as he did. What would make a guy do something like that, knowing full well the odds would cost him his life?

Years earlier General Douglas MacArthur had answered a similar question with these words:

> The soldier, above all other men, is required to practice the greatest act of religious training—sacrifice. In battle and in the face of danger and death, he discloses those divine attributes which his Maker gave when he created man in his own image. No physical courage and no brute instinct can take the place of the Divine help which alone can sustain him.[6]

I asked Dad if Doug was just one more kid who got caught up in some kind of emotional groundswell during the war, only to die like so much flotsam and jetsam washed up on some beach. Did it really matter? Dad responded with words to this effect: "No, Doug knew what he was doing. He was a thinker, a Christian kid who thought about life (and death) in large terms. As a believer, Doug had the big picture." Doug Munro prized our nation's founding ethic and our freedom. He personified the following statement by historian Stephen Ambrose:

> At the core, the American citizen-soldiers knew the difference between right and wrong, and they didn't want to live in a world in which wrong prevailed. So they fought, and won, and we all of us, living and yet to be born, must be forever profoundly grateful.[7]

I, for one, am very grateful that Doug didn't want to live in a world where wrong prevailed. And I'll tell all the marines out there that there was one young marine lieutenant colonel at Guadalcanal on that September 27 who was especially grateful for Doug Munro and men like him. He was the battalion commander of the marine unit Doug rescued. His name was Chesty Puller, the legend of the USMC who lived on to receive five Navy Crosses. Chesty and those marines, as well as you and me, owe our lives and freedom to the Doug Munros of this country.

I guess you could say Doug Munro and his ilk stimulated me as a boy to begin to see things a little more clearly—that life wasn't easy, that freedom isn't free. I read everything I could get my hands on that related to hard challenges and war and freedom. The "comic" books of my childhood treated the Korean War. But they weren't comical. They were filled with strong stories of sacrifice. The eyes of my heart, incredibly immature at the time, were at least beginning to envision life's realities on this tumultuous planet. There is such a thing as raw, cruel evil. Absolute evil.

Doug's story was significant for me. The big picture began to take root in my boyhood soul. And it went a little deeper when I read of Nathan Hale or Sam Adams (and later, Sam Whittemore).

I watched Disney's version of Davy Crockett and was enamored by a man who would travel a long distance, at personal expense and great risk, to help other folks like the Texans who were getting the slats kicked out of their lives. My eyes focused a little more.

Then came the 1960s.

When I hit college in the fall of 1963, Vietnam was hardly a blip on our horizon. But the next year or so I read in *Life* magazine of a young Green Beret by the name of Roger Donlon (a man I'm humbled today to count among my personal friends) who received that same Medal of Honor for his actions at a place called Nam Dong.

By my sophomore year we'd become much more aware of Vietnam. Despite the antiwar protests of some of our peers (and at least one family member who fled to Canada to avoid military service), it was no big problem for me to sign up for Army ROTC. That fall we learned that one of the guys on the football team who had recently graduated, a guy we all appreciated, had died that summer as a marine lieutenant in Vietnam. My eyes got a little sharper.

THE QUESTIONS OF TRANSCENDENT CAUSE

On army maneuvers in Germany during the summer of 1969 we gathered around the one available television set to watch our guys land on the moon. That same week I got my orders to Vietnam. In the spring of 1970 at a Special Forces A Camp in the Dak Poko Valley of the Central Highlands, I experienced my own "crowded hour." For the first time, at age twenty-four, it occurred to me in neon letters that I might die there. That one Stuart Weber might end his earthly existence within mere moments.

That's when what I call the questions of transcendent cause began to whirl through my mind. And soul. Do you ask yourself these questions along the way? I believe they are necessary to maintaining purpose and focus in a world that tends to erode both.

Why? Why am I alive? Why am I alive when others died? What actually happens after death? If I do die, what will it matter that I've actually lived? What difference does it make that I've ever been on this earth? What am I living for? What am I willing to die for, to spend myself for?

The eyes of my heart were getting keen. I was seeing with more clarity. Though intellectually I'd long ago abandoned my parents' faith, over a period of months the spiritual roots of my childhood heart began to sink deep and grow rapidly. I began to shape my direction and determine my life course "as it was in my heart," to use Caleb's phrase. As I was faced with choices, my decisions began to take on a spiritual undergirding.

A new clarity provided rejuvenating direction—I needed to become grounded in the very Word and words of God. For me, the Bible began to take on a life of its own. The values and interests of the living God, the Creator to whom our Founding Fathers appealed for humanity's unalienable rights, began to become my own values and interests. I'd never had any truly serious interest in organized religion or even in religion at all for that matter. But the pilgrimage of my soul in Vietnam and its wake explains some forty years of my life, so far, committed to live for my Lord, the High King of heaven, and for His kingdom. I'm still not "religious" in some kind of rule-oriented Pharisaical sense, and I am embarrassed by many of the religious professionals claiming to represent the Bible. I fear, as is often said, that Christ's cause is done more harm by His friends than His enemies. But I am fully and personally committed to the Creator-King of the universe.

It's that same Lord and that same kingdom that governed the conversation around that campfire some 3,500 years ago. Caleb could see the kingdom Moses had told him and Joshua about. Let's return again to this conversation of two battle-scarred warriors looking afresh at life and discussing the questions of transcendent cause.

"As it was in my heart," Caleb had stated in Joshua 14:7. These are reasoned words from a seasoned warrior. Caleb had "been there and back"—several times. The old soldier had been the "boots on the ground," quite literally, for decades now. The stripes on his forearm ran together. In terms of respect and esteem from others, Caleb ranked somewhere between command sergeant major and field marshal. And now he's laying his heart on the table.

This was it. Staring them in the face was the final phase—and in some ways, the most difficult—of the invasion and occupation of Canaan. Like Tommy Franks in Iraq, Joshua had directed his mainline units on a "run and gun" charge through the land without slowing down for isolated pockets of resistance. You might call it the Thunder Road of the Bronze Age. And now it was time to finish it off, to face the toughest stuff—

a "slug fest," hand to hand,

in some of the most difficult terrain on the map,

against some of the enemy's most hardened warriors.

In such a moment, what was on Caleb's mind? How would Israel's commanders approach this most difficult conclusion?

Picture again the two lifelong battle buddies, Joshua and Caleb, sitting at the fire that night. Their options have been laid out. Now it's time for the veteran warrior to speak from the heart. The world was about to see what this legendary warrior was made of. And Caleb would not disappoint.

A question: Think back to Doug Munro. Why in the world would a guy do that? What matters to a guy in his early twenties who'll choose to die like that? What was it in Doug's soul that governed him to make such a sacrifice?

Or relate the same questions to Caleb at that midnight hour fireside. Why in the world would an old man who's already spent a soldierly lifetime with spear in hand want to go at it once more at his advanced age? Why not just let somebody else do it?

Why? In a word, because of *heart*. Because the warrior soul beat in Caleb's chest. Because the spirit of the warrior is everything. Because, in Caleb's words, this is "as it was in my heart"!

Thirty-five centuries later another military legend borrowed from the same warrior lexicon. Remember General Marshall's words: "The soldier's heart, the soldier's spirit, the soldier's soul, are everything"?[8] As Caleb delivered Israel in 1400 BC, so General Marshall would deliver Europe in the 1940s of the common era. In both soldiers' hearts there was that rhythm, that sense of transcendent cause. From the fireside in Canaan, to the outpost in Afghanistan, to the Pentagon—the warrior heart beats to a transcendent cause.

The ultimate transcendent cause is a personal belief in the God of righteousness and His Son, Jesus Christ. So it should come as no surprise that many of our young warriors in Iraq carried little dog tag-like shields inscribed with biblical words borrowed from Joshua: "I will be strong and courageous. I will not be terrified, or discouraged; for the Lord my God is with me wherever I go."

A sense of transcendent cause may be defined as having a singular heart for something larger than self—something to stand for, to struggle for, to sacrifice for. Caleb used that phrase, "as it was in my heart"; there was something beating deep in Caleb's chest. You can almost hear him saying, "Joshua, it's here in the core of my being. It's who I am. It's the air I breathe. It's what I live for, and what I'll die for. I carry it in my soul. It's a matter of deep conviction. I *believe* in this!"

BEYOND US

What do *you* believe? What really matters to you? Have you thought through your sense of transcendent cause? Whatever it is, it must be bigger than you are.

How big is it?

- Do you live for yourself? *Not good. Too small.*

- Do you live for your business, career, or making money? *Doesn't qualify. Money is no transcendent cause.*

- Do you live for your wife and family? *That's bigger. And somewhat better.*

- Do you live for your nation? Or, more vaguely, "humanity"? *That's transcendent. But it still falls short of ultimate transcendence.*

- Do you live for a principle, such as "freedom"? *That's good. But just what does it mean? Is it just temporal freedom? Political freedom? Freedom from foreign oppression? Individual freedom?*

The proverbial old instruction is, "Pick your hill to die on." You must think through, figure out, and actively decide what's important enough for you to defend with your life. Make it worth it!

What is your life about? What do you live for? What are you all about? Of course, as believers we understand Christ to be the ultimate transcendent cause! We'll come to that in a bit. But first let's take a walk with an actual, real-life soldier asking himself some transcendent questions in the midst of a very real battle.

For the soldier in a firefight, honestly, the transcendent cause of which he's aware at that moment may be no larger than the buddy in the ditch beside him. That's good enough in the heat of flying bullets. But eventually the more mature warrior has to identify and settle in on something larger—a principle, an abiding truth, a spiritual value by which he'll govern himself and his conduct.

Karl Marlantes, in his excellent book *What It Is Like to Go to War,* says it well:

> To be effective and moral fighters, we must not lose our individuality, our ability to stand alone; and yet, at the same time, we must owe our allegiance not to ourselves but to an entity so large as to be incomprehensible, namely, humanity or God.[9]

I couldn't agree more!

One Soldier's Vivid Journey

In fact, let me do something a bit unusual here and take a page or two to introduce you to this very real warrior, a man you should like and a book you should read.

Karl Marlantes graduated from Yale University in the sixties, was a Rhodes Scholar at Oxford, and then served in the United States Marine Corps in Vietnam in 1969 at the age of twenty-three. Slipping out of Oxford's highly academic doors, he wandered, long hair and all, somewhat aimlessly across Africa, trying to determine if he should keep his commitments to the Marine Corps and his country in a controversial conflict like Vietnam. It wasn't in him to back out, so he went. And his life, like those of so many young soldiers, would never be the same.

War changed Karl's life.

He emerged from a year in Vietnam still young but a different man. While he received a Navy Cross (second only to the Medal of Honor in the hierarchy of awards for battlefield valor), the Bronze Star, two Navy Commendation medals for valor, two Purple Hearts, and ten air medals, he also came home with a soul full of questions—the kind of questions that eventually make or break a man's character. They made Karl's.

In my eyes Karl's book, *What It Is Like to Go to War,* is both a tribute to, as well as a training manual for, the warrior soul. But it's far more than a manual. Written humbly and transparently, it's the journal of a mature man making sense of his younger warrior years. The writing is brilliant and insightful. One reviewer described it as "a staggeringly beautiful book on combat." Normally we wouldn't put the words "beautiful" and "combat" in the same paragraph, let alone the same phrase. In this case, it applies.

The reader experiences that rare but warming sense of having come to know the author on a first-name basis, even friend to friend. Karl states at the outset that he wrote the book to come to terms with his own combat experience. "So far...that has taken more than forty years."[10] *So far.* Yes, so long as we breathe the breath of life, soldiers will be sorting through the ultimates that are forced upon us in a combat environment.

I had already written much of *The Warrior Soul* when a friend referred me to Karl's book. While my own experiences in Vietnam don't even begin to approach the frequency and intensity of Karl's, I was repeatedly overcome, while reading his book, with the familiarity of my own similar questions and conclusions. Even some of the vocabulary was the same. I felt like I had come across a kindred spirit. Often, reading his book, I found myself repeatedly thinking, "Thanks, Karl, for helping us learn to walk that 'path of transcendence' as you call it."

Ultimates and *transcendence* are words that first began to dawn on me as a twenty-four-year-old on a Hawaiian beach while on R&R from Vietnam. I had survived some time in Vietnam's deadly Dak Poko valley, and now I was in "paradise" with my bride. My head was spinning. Two worlds so very far apart, but separated by one relatively brief jet ride. You've already read the questions that once troubled my soul: Why am I alive? And why are others not? And what does it matter that I'm alive?

Life and death are ultimate issues. When death is no longer theoretical, life begins to seek its focus. Our souls strive to find themselves. That greatest of human traits—spiritual perspective—begins to take shape. We begin to thirst for an ultimately transcendent explanation, something much larger than ourselves. Not surprisingly, but quite rightly, that spiritual journey eventually gravitates toward something of religious tone. There are reasons for that.

Karl insightfully depicts a soldier's baptism in combat as his entry into "the temple of Mars" (not the planet, of course, but the dwelling place of the classical Greek god of war). Karl rightly describes combat as entering into "wartime sacred space." He personalizes his own violent introduction to the temple of Mars, explains that the Marine Corps taught him how to kill but not how to deal with killing. He says he lost his sense of where he was spiritually and speaks of his once instinctive link to the spiritual world being "finally severed by military training,"[11] which had unintentionally omitted the spiritual. I had to nod knowingly, as I'm sure many other veterans did, at such insightful descriptors!

Karl's response to combat is spiritually perceptive. As he engaged in killing and the possibility of being killed, he writes, "I needed help with the existential terror of my own death and responsibility for the death of others, enemies and friends. . . . I needed a spiritual guide."[12]

Karl thoughtfully defends his rightful insistence (and that of Boykin and myself) that war is, at its very root, ultimately a spiritual experience:

> Consider this. Mystical or religious experiences have four common components: constant awareness of one's own inevitable death, total focus on the present moment, the valuing of other people's lives above one's own, and being part of a larger . . . community. . . . All four of these exist in combat. The big difference is that the mystic sees heaven and the warrior sees hell.[13]

Well said! He goes on to say that many of us like to think of a sacred space as a place where we can feel good.

> We don't want to think that something as ugly and brutal as combat could be involved in any way with the spiritual. However, would any practicing Christian say that Calvary Hill was not a sacred space?[14]

Thank you, Karl; you're right again. In fact, in an ultimate sense, virtually *everything* in life has something to do with spiritual reality.

At the time of my own introduction to the temple of Mars, I didn't know for sure what a practicing Christian actually was. Now

I do. My own struggling journey down the "path of transcendence" led me to Christ in a very personal way. I now fully believe there's no more beauty-filled place on Earth than the high ground of Calvary where the battle of the ages took place between the Champion of heaven, Jesus Christ, and that evil denizen of hell itself—Satan, the adversary of our souls.

Calvary, the centerpiece of the Bible and that to which every biblical story and major character points, is the scene of the most outlandish combat in history. You already read in earlier pages in this book that the first note of that gigantic battle is on virtually page one of the Bible, Genesis 3. And that the first hint of Messiah (the Hebrew term for Christ) pictures Him as a wounded warrior, struck on the heel. And that in the process of His own wounding (which ultimately could not keep Him in the grave) the Messiah dealt an eternally lethal wound to Satan's head. You already know that a final picture of Jesus in Scripture has Him mounted on a white war horse, wearing a blood-splattered robe and wielding a sword with which He both launches and terminates the actual "war to end all wars." But that's another book. (You may wish to read one I wrote a decade ago on this theme, *Spirit Warriors*.)

As Karl says so well, soldiers are deeply involved with suffering and responsibility, because they're causing a lot of it. "Warriors must touch their souls because their job involves killing people," he writes. "Warriors deal with eternity."[15]

Karl adds that his "lessons in eternity weren't over yet,"[16] and that's a wise reminder for all of us.

Before we finish here with his fine book, let me pass along this comment of his about his experience in boot camp:

> There was one very critical issue that was missing from this particular passage of mine—the spiritual. I did connect with something larger than myself, the Marine Corps, but that is a

long way from connecting with something larger than myself such as humanity or God.

You have to love this man's thoughtful insight and utter honesty! And his accuracy. He wisely understands that the only healthy way to deal with the horrible realities of combat is by finding a path of transcendence. One must get above it in order to survive it, let alone understand it. He has rightly chosen to avoid some simplistic (though seemingly esoteric) descriptor for the transcendent, and instead rightly insists on personifying the ultimate transcendence, as he perceives it—either humanity or God. I believe he's quite right...as far as he goes.

There's yet one more absolutely crucial step. That transcendent God has a name, a very personal name.

The Bible describes humanity as the *imago Dei*, or "image of God," which separates mankind from "the beasts of the field." The human being enjoys what we might call "personhood"—that divine image none of the rest of creation bears similarly. The central point of imago Dei is, of course, the *Dei*—God Himself. The human being is a creature who longs to know and be known, to love and be loved, to trust and be trusted. It's all a reflection of that image of God.

Marlantes is right to ground his sense of transcendence in its highest forms. Humanity transcends the animal kingdom. And God transcends humanity. His personal name is Jesus.

The central purpose of the Bible is to reveal the ultimate Transcendent One—that Person of God—to us humans, who now are desperately fallen since Eden. Jesus, our Redeemer-Warrior, is the ultimate "image of the invisible God." Bottom line, Jesus *is* God, the Creator God, the ultimate Transcendent One. "By Him all things were created, both in the heavens and on earth, visible and invisible...all things have been created through Him and for Him. He is before all things, and in Him all things hold together" (Col. 1:15–17).

Everything truly noble about humanity is downstream from Jesus.

The explicit claim of Scripture is that Jesus is God incarnate. Unlike the founders or leaders of other world religions, Jesus's claims are outrageously exclusive. So much so, they force us, as ultimates always do, to a choice: *Is Jesus right or wrong?* And Jesus leaves us no wiggle room. Normal humans don't talk as Jesus did. People are locked up in insane asylums for speaking as He did: "I am the way, and the truth, and the life....He who believes in Me will live even if he dies" (John 14:6; 11:25). And those are just for starters. Great moral teachers don't talk like that—unless they are who they claim to be.

No, Jesus was either the "Lord, a liar, or a lunatic," as others have summed it up. If He was wrong and didn't know it, He was just crazy; if He was wrong and *did* know it, He's just one more in a long line of con artists. He would be, as C. S. Lewis so well stated, "on the level with the man who says he is a poached egg, or else he would be the Devil of Hell." Or—He is Lord and God. Lewis concludes, "But let us not come up with any patronizing nonsense about His being a great human teacher. He has not left that option open to us. He did not intend to."[17]

Jesus, the suffering Savior and Lamb of God, is also the victorious Lion of Judah who will return to rule the world. Jesus is the greatest warrior who ever lived, having conquered at Calvary the ruler of this present darkness, Satan himself. The battle on that sacred high ground at Calvary was the D-Day of all time.

Christ's victory on Calvary was declared not with a headline but with a resurrection! And that victory determined the outcome of the war. The turmoil we experience today amounts to "mopping up" operations on the heels of D-Day. Ultimate victory in "Eden" is just around the corner!

Yes, meet God. His name is Jesus. And He happens to love you, very personally. Again, if you read nothing else in this book, read the last chapter with an open mind and heart.

YES, BEYOND US!

A transcendent cause is a mission that lifts us beyond ourselves, a passion that stirs us to self-sacrifice and causes us to contribute to something much larger than ourselves. To put it in simple terms, every man among us wants his life to count for something important. It may be his friends, his wife, his family, his country, or his faith.

Sociologist Ernest Becker expressed it this way:

> Man will lay down his life for his country, his society, his family. He will choose to throw himself on a grenade to save his comrades; he is capable of the highest generosity and self-sacrifice. But he has to feel and believe that what he is doing is truly heroic, timeless, and supremely meaningful.[18]

Think about those closing words. *Supremely meaningful.* The word *supreme* points us to what is first, top, best, highest. *Meaning* indicates what is significant, critical, important, invaluable. *Timeless* speaks of going beyond the present moment to the long haul—and beyond that as well to what's eternal.

And *heroic*? Sacrificing for others is at the core of the heroic. It is also at the core of the Christian life, is it not?

Believer, can you see that owning Christ as your transcendent cause enables you to view and value everything in your life—both the mundane and the monumental—as supremely meaningful?

Surely every Christian warrior understands that Christ is the ultimate transcendent cause. The apostle Paul said as much in multiple scriptures. Here are just some of the more obvious instances:

> Whatever you do, do all to the glory of God.
> —1 CORINTHIANS 10:31

> For to me, to live is Christ.
> —PHILIPPIANS 1:21

> Conduct yourselves in a manner worthy of the gospel of
> Christ.
>
> —PHILIPPIANS 1:27

For us believing warriors, Christ is so transcendent that *everything* is about Him and not us. Christ figures in *everything*. He is the reason we live and breathe. Even basic physical functions such as eating and drinking (1 Cor. 10:31) are done to His glory. Living is about Christ. Dying is about Christ. The Christian warrior does all things in light of who Christ is.

Since my marriage is not about me, I can sacrifice my life for my wife. Since nothing is about us, and everything is about Him, we really can/must/should "do all things through Him who strengthens" us (Phil. 4:13).

Since my job is not about me, I can do it as unto the Lord and quit complaining.

Since my life is not about me, I can willingly die for Him and His cause.

It is this quality of sacrifice—derived from a sense of transcendent cause—that drives and energizes us in the battles, both large and small, we face every day of our lives. To put it back in the physical warrior's world of sacrifice, see if you can identify with the principles and values in the following discussion. While the conversation is fictitious, its meaning is not. It takes place in ancient Sparta, somewhere around 480 BC, not far from the shadows of the towering cliffs at Thermopylae.

Stephen Pressfield's historical novel *Gates of Fire* gives account of the famous Spartan victory over the Persians. Three hundred noble soldiers, to save their city, marched deliberately to their death at a narrow pass near thermal springs—the "gates of fire." They were the product of a military culture in the city-state of Sparta that was legendary for training every male to be a warrior, beginning at age fourteen.

In his novel Pressfield relates a conversation between a young

Spartan trainee and his seasoned mentor. It had been a particularly grueling day, with one young man killed in a training accident. His peers saw death for the first time. It's a moment that the mentor, Dienekes, makes the most of:

> Such is the peculiar genius of the Spartan system of pairing each youngster in training with a mentor other than his own father. A mentor may say things that a father cannot....
>
> "It was a bad day today, wasn't it, my young friend?" Dienekes then asked the boy how he imagined battle, real battle, compared with what he had witnessed today.
>
> No answer was required or expected.
>
> "Never forget, Alexandros, that this flesh, this body, does not belong to us. Thank God it doesn't. If I thought this was mine, I could not advance a pace into the face of the enemy. But it is not ours, my friend. It belongs to the gods and to our children, our fathers and mothers and those...a hundred, a thousand years yet unborn. It belongs to the city which gives us all we have and demands no less in requital."[19]

The Spartan conviction was that one's life belonged to the gods, their families, and their city. (Or as we might say it, God, family, and country.)

That's a transcendent cause—to a point. And we must never forget it! For even that worthy transcendent cause of the Spartans falls short of the ultimate—an eternal value and identity. Ultimately, of course, there's only one ultimate, and He is Christ. If you've not yet identified with Him—the Creator God—I urge you to do so before you finish this book. (Let me mention again that in chapter 13, you'll meet the greatest warrior who ever lived...the eternal Son of God, Jesus Christ. Don't be caught dead without Him!)

A Present Gratitude

Meanwhile, in the present moment, aware of our own military services, be sure you thank God for our freedom and those in uniform who secure it.

I hope the great bulk of Americans today are extremely grateful for the men and women of our own US military services, past and present, who have courageously acted in sacrificial fashion. In my family the gratitude is never far from our minds.

I recall a day, not all that long ago, when my wife and I and two of our adult sons and their children were having a great day, unforgettably pleasant. The sun shone in a blue sky as we wandered through Seattle's Woodland Park Zoo. The little kids' eyes lit up at every turn. There was adventure and joy in every step that day.

At one point my daughter-in-law Carolyn stopped us and made a magnificent suggestion. She gathered all the kids around and said something like this: "As we're here skipping along in freedom and joy, our soldiers are on the other side of the earth working very hard, in the heat of the desert and the danger of combat, to keep us free. There's no terrorist bomb in Woodland Park Zoo today because our brave men and women in the military are watching out for us. Let's thank God for their service and our freedom."

I have to admit, my eyes glazed over, and the eyes of my heart swelled with gratitude for our troops—and for my daughter-in-law, who "gets it."

Something More, Something Higher

Transcendent—that's a fifty-cent word with a million-dollar meaning, which is why a transcendent cause must be something more significant than money or pleasure or lifestyle or possessions. It's got to be about principles, values, standards. Abiding principles, absolute values, and enduring standards. Things that don't change with time or with personal or cultural whim. Eternal things.

Ultimately it must be about knowing God.

That's the point—it's transcendent. Down inside. Deep in the chest. In the character. It has everything to do with personal, authentic humanity created in the image of God.

Soldiers must learn to believe in something larger than themselves. It's part of the warrior's code, the culture of sacrifice, a determination to be *free*—free to pursue a vision, free to do the right thing. And it comes with a determination to provide that same freedom to others. Mature warriors understand, as the Bible constantly affirms, that there's no such thing as freedom apart from sacrifice.

It's the character of the warrior soul that carries the day.

That's precisely why the US military touts the motto: *Building leaders of character for the nation.*

And that's why West Point's Cadet Prayer—written in 1924 and still studied today—is what it is:

> O God, our Father, Thou Searcher of human hearts, help us to draw near to Thee in sincerity and truth. May our religion be filled with gladness and may our worship of Thee be natural.
>
> Strengthen and increase our admiration for honest dealing and clean thinking, and suffer not our hatred of hypocrisy and pretence ever to diminish. Encourage us in our endeavor to live above the common level of life. Make us to choose the harder right instead of the easier wrong, and never to be content with a half truth when the whole can be won. Endow us with courage that is born of loyalty to all that is noble and worthy, that scorns to compromise with vice and injustice and knows no fear when truth and right are in jeopardy. Guard us against flippancy and irreverence in the sacred things of life. Grant us new ties of friendship and new opportunities of service. Kindle our hearts in fellowship with those of a cheerful countenance, and soften our hearts with sympathy for those who sorrow

and suffer. Help us to maintain the honor of the Corps untarnished and unsullied and to show forth in our lives the ideals of West Point in doing our duty to Thee and to our Country. All of which we ask in the name of the Great Friend and Master of all.

Amen.[20]

That Great Friend and Master has a personal name, very personal—Jesus!

The superintendent of the United States Military Academy, Lieutenant General F. L. Hagenbeck, described this prayer's impact upon him personally:

> This humble fragment of military lore has become a transcendent didactic and cultural force here at the Academy. Its moral precepts have inspired and guided generations of West Point graduates in peace and war, and continue to do so to this day, including, with all humility, myself.[21]

That's why West Point, in developing leaders of character, utilizes the book *Forging the Warrior's Character: Moral Precepts from the Cadet Prayer.*[22] And it's why General Eric Shinseki (34th US Army chief of staff, retired 2003) writes this:

> Throughout my 38 years as a soldier, the responsibilities of leadership were underscored time and again by the words of the Cadet Prayer—words I was inspired by when I first heard them 46 years ago. They remind us that ethics is about the unwavering demand of duty…understanding the difference between right and wrong, and then doing what is right without fail.[23]

The spiritual and moral concepts so critical to right soldiering are captured in the "Army Values" to be understood, memorized, and enacted by every soldier: "Loyalty, Duty, Respect, Selfless Service, Honor, Integrity, Personal Courage."[24]

Though Caleb never recited that list at West Point, he knew, understood, and owned every one of those qualities.

SELF-EVIDENT TRUTHS

Talk about a transcendent cause! This United States of America is founded on one.

Sure enough, in a firefight, that immediate transcendent cause isn't much larger than the buddy next to you in the foxhole. In quieter, more reflective moments the cause gradually enlarges—to one's wife and family, to his community, "and to the republic" for which that flag stands. For the mature warrior, over more time and reflection, that transcendent cause will come to rest in values, in abiding principles, in transcendent matters, like these, for instance:

> We hold these truths to be self-evident, that all men are created equal, that they are endowed by their Creator with certain inalienable Rights....
>
> We therefore...appealing to the Supreme Judge of the world for the rectitude of our intentions...with a firm reliance on the protection of divine Providence, we mutually pledge to each other our Lives, our Fortunes, and our sacred Honor.[25]

Not unlike Caleb, our nation's forefathers believed certain things and were willing to live for them, suffer for them, and if necessary die for them. As we see in the Declaration of Independence just quoted, our nation's founders were believing and acting upon decidedly theological, spiritual, and yes, religious notions.

In every generation of Americans there are those who have stood up to act upon the same beliefs—from Lexington to Lang Vei...from Trenton to Tora Bora...from the halls of Montezuma to the shores of Tripoli...from the sands of Iraq to the ridges of Afghanistan. Those who serve today in the United States military stand on the able shoulders of those who have gone before.

How about you and me, as Christians living in America by God's sovereign design? (See Acts 17:26.) Can we take it upon ourselves to intensify our efforts to put those "self-evident truths" back in the forefront of our cultural lives? The battle for our culture is an ever-widening, ever-deepening struggle. We all sense it fast approaching the tipping point. America desperately needs a spiritual revival and what our founders called "a frequent recurrence to fundamentals." That's what this next chapter is all about.

Stay strong. Stay faithful. Stay focused on the transcendent. Pursue the only ultimate transcendent one, Jesus Christ. And stay in the fight.

☆ Chapter 6 ☆

A SETTLED MEMORY

The Sheer Power of History Remembered

If you dwell in the past you lose an eye. If
your forget the past you lose both eyes.[1]
• ANCIENT NEAR EASTERN PROVERB •

I FORGOT!"

I think that may have been the mantra of my childhood. At least it was my favorite alibi for failing at some responsibility. My parents responded much as yours probably did: "Forgetting is no excuse. In the right situation, it could cost you your life..."or some other seemingly inflated form to make their point unforgettable. Like so many great principles this one flew over the top of my youthful head. Not anymore!

Memory is an amazing human capacity, perhaps exceeded only by our capacity to forget. And, yes, forgetting can get you killed. Nobody wins with forgetfulness. Everyone loses.

Whoever said "history is the past" was short-sighted at best and foolish at worst. The past is not even past. It stares us in the face every day. We're all familiar with the greatest lesson of history— that those who forget it are doomed to repeat it. So very true.

Here's but one clear and large-scale example that is impacting your life today: *World War I.*

"Whoa, come on!" you say. "That was forever ago, like a century!"

Yes, it was. And its lessons are as fresh today as they were in 1918. Our global maps today still reflect the fallout of World War I. World War I was supposedly the war to end all wars. That was the most popular so-called lesson coming out of the horror of slaughter in the trenches: *That was so bad it could never happen again.* And because both leaders and populace believed there could never be another such war, at least on that scale, they fell asleep at the wheel—only to be jarred awake in 1939 with the world on fire again.

Hitler had begun preparing for World War II on November 11, 1918, Armistice Day, the day World War I "ended." On that same day the young corporal heard Germany had been defeated and shamed. He determined to see that Germany would rise from the ashes and dominate the world. World War II was a direct result of World War I.

So how did it go after the war to end all wars? Well, the twentieth century would become the bloodiest by far in human history. Scores of millions were killed.

And here's a great irony. The leader of the free world who forgot history on the heels of World War I was what we sometimes call today a humanities professor! American president Woodrow Wilson was a career academician and political scientist, but he failed to visualize history. He forgot a rather key point. In blatant human naïveté he believed mankind (as it seems many who call themselves "progressives" believe today) had learned its lesson and changed for the good. The world was now "safe for democracy." So how are we doing now a century later? Do you feel safe today? How is democracy doing worldwide?

Wilson believed in a global economy, in the rule of enlightened reason, in the goodness of man, in the progress of technology, and in the dialogue of a League of Nations, where human beings could sit down and become one big, happy family. It's not going to happen. Not on this old earth. Not in this life. If history teaches us one thing, it is that we humans are utter failures at governing ourselves. Oh, our "enlightened scientific education" may have added a few years to our average lifespan, but that same education has enabled us to kill one another in greater "wholesale" numbers than ever before—both before and after birth. The twentieth century was the bloodiest century of all time. Talk about being on the wrong side of history. That's our world today.

History clearly teaches us that some things never change—human nature, for one. We may advance in technology, in science, in the arts, in psychology, in sociology, in communication, in...you name it. But apart from supernatural intervention, our hearts and souls never change. We only become more effective at taking advantage of one another. We shouldn't be surprised that war is likely the single greatest constant in human history. And that's a lesson from history no one should forget. We have it on good authority there will always be wars and rumors of war.

THE PERSONAL LEVEL

What about you and me, warriors on the ground? What about little old us? Is remembering important on a personal level?

The consequences of forgetting are tragic at every level—individual, marital, familial, regional, national, and international. Those who forget will wallow in a miserably repetitive cycle. Welcome to the human condition.

That's why no one insists more emphatically upon the power of settled memory than God Himself. The Bible is replete with directives reinforcing the absolute necessity that we remember. I like to call it the doctrine of remembrance. You certainly won't find it listed in any systematic theologies, and it's not a course in seminary. But it is essential, even critical, to a healthy warrior soul. You may want to pick up a copy of a book I wrote previously, *Infinite Impact*.[2] It's an entire book on this topic of the power of remembrance alone. I've reflected some of its content in the paragraphs below.

"I shall remember the deeds of the LORD," writes the psalmist

Asaph. "I will remember [His] wonders of old...and muse on [them]...teach them...and not forget the works of God" (Ps. 77:11–12; 78:5–7).

Just before our God took Caleb and Israel into the Promised Land, He sat them down in the desert and gave them a straightforward lesson with a hard slap to the blackboard:

> All the commandments that I am commanding you today you shall be careful to do....You shall remember all the way which the LORD your God has led you in the wilderness....Beware that you do not forget the LORD your God...[or] your heart will become proud....But you shall remember the LORD your God...and if you ever forget...you will surely perish.
> —DEUTERONOMY 8:1–2, 11, 14, 18–19

Remembering. God insisted on it; without it man is a helpless vagrant wandering aimlessly on a planet that is disintegrating. God insists we remember—from one end of the Bible to the other. Remember. Never forget. In the Old Testament books of the law, history, poetry, and prophets, and throughout the New Testament, the voice of the Almighty speaks to this priority again and again. "You must remember!" It's as close to a mantra as anything in the Bible.

In the Old Testament the Hebrew words translated "memory," "remember," or "remembrance" are all related to a single root word: *zakar* The word *zakar* refers to a multifaceted process: (1) mentally bringing something to mind, (2) the reflection inherent in that mindfulness, and (3) the corresponding behavioral act appropriate to that memory. In other words, to remember biblically is *to recall-reflect-react*. Remembering isn't just a passing thought about the past. To remember biblically is to think, to reflect, and to act all in singular process. It is so much more than not forgetting.

If we fail to remember, we will pay a heavy price. Here's one very real current example. Few things in our modern day represent a larger, more horrific battle than the role of the Middle East in world affairs. Our twenty-first century opened with the world's attention riveted on the events of 9/11 and the *seemingly* new threat of terrorism. The lack of peace in the Middle East surfaces in some ugly form every week of our lives today. And we Americans wander around in a cloud of confusion like this is something new.

Remember the headlines, "Why do they hate us so?" The answer, while not hard to discern, seems difficult for people to swallow. Bottom-line, historic Islam and its most ardent adherents—known variously as Islamic fundamentalists, Islamic jihadists, or Islamic extremists—have always been fundamentally hostile to any other worldview. Islam is so much more than a religion. It is a totalitarian ideology governing all of life—economics, politics, ethics, religion, and more.

Historically one would have to admit that Osama bin Laden was a good Muslim. Yes, there are many "moderate" Muslims who don't share the violent worldview. Most "moderate" Muslims don't practice the historic Islam all that well. (Similarly, many "mainline Christian" denominations don't believe in some historic Christian fundamentals such as the deity of Christ or His bodily resurrection.) The point is this—violent Islam is not new. We have simply failed to remember, and that could get us killed.

So, Christian warrior, develop your memory muscle. Work it out every day. Remembering may be the most important exercise you will ever practice. Discipline the "settled memory" of your biblical warrior soul. Virtually everything of spiritual consequence depends upon memory. In forgetting our souls shrink, our dreams wither, our hearts break, and Christ's kingdom suffers.

Listen to the swan song of one of the great warriors of the New Testament and take note of all the memory-related words:

> I shall not fail to *remind* you of things like this although you know them and are *already established* in the truth. I consider it my *duty, as long as I live* in the temporary dwelling of

this body, to *stimulate* you by these reminders. I know that I shall have to leave this body at very short notice, as our Lord Jesus Christ made clear to me. Consequently I shall *make the most* of every opportunity, so that *after I am gone* you will *remember* these things.

—2 PETER 1:12–15, PHILLIPS

So what can you personally do about all this? *Choose to remember!* Memory (yes, history!) is a great gift of God to enable us to learn from the past, to live well today, and to plan effectively for the future.

That's precisely what Caleb is doing in our campfire conversation. It's especially incumbent on a warrior never to forget. Listen to Caleb's conversation with Joshua. The old soldier continually made reference to the past, in order to think clearly in the present, so they could plan future operations. His words in Joshua 14 are laced with remembering—reflecting, reminding, rethinking. He repeatedly reminds Joshua of the past, of God's Word, of His kingdom promises, of the covenant land, of former battles, of lessons learned. This warrior is well schooled across the board—in personal history (he reminds Joshua that his years have been strenuous); in military history (he mentions that his operational experiences are as fresh as the morning); in family history (based on the past, he envisions the heritage he'll leave behind).

Most importantly Caleb is well versed in theological history. *He knows God*—the character of God, the Word of God, the faithfulness of God, and the guidance of God. This guy is kitted up for battle at any and every level. Caleb is "fit to fight." And he's chosen very well the hill to die on. It's the mountaintop of God's calling for his life—the ultimate transcendent cause!

So let's take a closer look at the power of this "remembering" thing.

You must remember! Those are some of the most potent words in our language. Forget to shave or brush your teeth—no big deal, only temporarily embarrassing. Forget to take your medicine—slightly more serious. Forget to turn off the stove—you may burn your house down. But, most potently, if you forget the lessons of the past, you'll suffer in the present as well as destroy your future.

FOUNDED ON HISTORY

God has placed us believers here on this planet with a citizenship in heaven and a responsibility as citizens on Earth. He actually instructed His earthly people to "seek the welfare of the [nation] where I have sent you... for in its welfare you will have welfare" (Jer. 29:7). Now, if God so instructs His people dragged off into captivity by a pagan culture worshipping a plethora of false gods, how much more should we, living in a nation with an explicit Judeo-Christian heritage, take it to heart?

Our Founding Fathers were historical thinkers. That's a momentous message for America today. Our Founding Fathers studied the past—the nature of God, the nature of man, the forms of civic governance, and the history of empires. Out of that historical intelligence they created a nation unique among the family of nations.

And what did they focus on in their study of the past?

Theological history

Our founders studied the history of theology, the Bible, and the understanding of the nature of God. And they made regular reference to it.

Our nation's birth certificate, the US Declaration of Independence, is based on a decidedly theological notion. The founders held certain theological principles to be so utterly true that they declared them "self-evident"—so true that they didn't countenance any debate or argument, and any fool could grasp their realities. Those principles stated that humans are "created"; that humans are "created equal"; that they're "endowed by their Creator [yes, with a capital C in the original document] with certain unalienable rights,"

rights that are not derived from Washington, DC, or any other earthly government or authority.

Our founders also regarded freedom as a sacred and righteous cause; they therefore appealed to God, "the Supreme Judge," and expressed their "firm reliance on the protection of divine Providence" for their cause and its sustenance.

Given those convictions, they were willing to die on the hill of their Declaration: "We mutually pledge to each other our lives, our fortunes, and our sacred honor."

Now those were some kind of men! Newsman Tom Brokaw labeled the people of my dad's era as "the greatest generation," and he did so for many good reasons. Nevertheless, I believe the generation of our founders was truly our greatest.

Our revolutionary warriors fought under flags bearing such mottos as "An Appeal to Heaven" and "An Appeal to God." The Pennsylvanians fought under a flag whose motto was to become the familiar battle cry of the American Revolution: "Resistance to Tyrants Is Obedience to God." Even the popular songs of the day—"The Liberty Song" and "American Hearts of Oak"—rehearsed their common belief that "Heaven approves of each generous deed...for Providence always defends the oppressed."[3] Our founders believed, according to their own words in the Declaration, that the major purpose of our national government was to "secure these rights" that are sourced in God.

Whew! We've fallen a long ways from our founding, haven't we? We've forgotten our roots; we've lost sight of where we came from as well as where we were originally headed. It is succinctly stated in these words, attributed to Solzhenitsyn: "To destroy a people, you must first sever their roots!"[4]

You likely saw the movie *The Lion King*. The once thriving and luxuriant kingdom was destitute because the young lion-leader was lost and wandering in a wilderness much of his own making. He had forgotten. The entire film turns on a single scene. At the "pool of reflection," the discouraged and failed lion-leader stares into the waters. He sees reflected there the great father-leaders of the past, and he hears their single voice and repeated message: "Remember who you are! Remember who you are!"[5] The young lion comes to his senses, remembers his roots, and returns to the ways of the fathers. *America, take a lesson!*

We must *never* forget. Our great Founding Father George Washington himself longed for us to remember. During his first term as president he stated publicly:

> I am sure there never was a people who had more reason to acknowledge a divine interposition in their affairs, than those of the United States, and I should be pained to believe that they have forgotten that agency, which was so often manifested during our revolution, or that they failed to consider the omnipotence of that God who alone is able to protect them.[6]

Human culture and society

Our founders also studied the history of the nature of man and the history of human empires. And they determined to *learn* from that history.

Equally astounding as the Declaration of Independence, the US Constitution is utterly unique among the nations of history. The founders understood that human nature is perpetually corrupted, that men always seek power more than freedom, and that we're prone to the tyranny of our own selfish interests. "There is a danger from all men," John Adams wrote. "The only maxim of a free government ought to be to trust no living man with power to endanger public liberty."[7] So the founders formed a constitutional republic complete with checks and balances of power—in order to protect us from ourselves!

Benjamin Franklin understood our human propensity. When asked what kind of government the founders had established in their deliberations, he famously replied, "A republic, if you can keep it."[8]

Our Founding Fathers, as with so much of their vocabulary, had a rather quaint way of referring to the necessity of remembering. They called it a necessary and "frequent recurrence to fundamentals."[9] General Krulak, former Marine Corps commandant, called them "moral touchstones"[10] on the path of freedom.

The army works at it as well. In the late 1990s, at the annual conference of the army's senior four-star generals, the agenda was tightly managed around thirty-minute decision briefings. But one of those half-hour sessions broke out of its time frame and dominated the conference. One of the generals in attendance said it felt as though "time stood still" for over three hours as the generals confronted one another over a single topic.[11]

The subject? *Morality and values.*

These senior four-star warriors were vitally concerned about the moral fiber of the army. It seems as though today's young recruits were coming into the military out of an American culture that has lost touch with its moral roots. Our eighteen- to twenty-year-olds had lost touch with our earlier culture's long-standing "moral touchstones." The generals understood that one cannot place modern weaponry into any pair of hands that aren't self-governed by thoughtfully developed moral values. So those generals set about the mission of identifying, defining, and implementing training around the "Army values." Taken together, the first letter of each forms an acrostic to represent LDRSHIP:

- *Leadership*—Bear true faith and allegiance to the US Constitution, the Army, your unit, and other Soldiers.

- *Duty*—Fulfill your obligations.

- *Respect*—Treat people as they should be treated.

- *Selfless Service*—Put the welfare of the nation, the Army, and your subordinates before your own.

- *Honor*—Live up to Army values.

- *Integrity*—Do what's right, legally and morally.

- *Personal Courage*—Face fear, danger, or adversity (physical or moral).[12]

Each of the definitions is expanded to form a fabric that will build the warrior's character and enhance his capacity as an individual, married and family person, and citizen soldier.

The generals were discovering what the Founding Fathers had stated two centuries prior. John Adams addressed the very same issue. Writing to officers of the First Brigade, Third Massachusetts Division, Adams declared:

> We have no government…capable of contending with human passions unbridled by morality and religion. Avarice, ambition, revenge…would break the strongest cords of our Constitution as a whale goes through a net. Our Constitution was made only for a moral and religious people. It is wholly inadequate to the government of any other.[13]

It is man's nature to forget history and its lessons and values, and in so doing to lose his way. Our founders would roll in their graves if they could see the unconstitutional abuse of power in our nation today. They would take any number of our current leaders to the woodshed and do some serious slapping.

ANCHORED

Back to Caleb. The man couldn't get history out of his mind. This man could therefore see with more than the eyes in his head. He could envision with the eyes of his heart. And, boy, did he *see*. Caleb got it.

He couldn't stop talking about history, let alone forget it. He remembered who he was, he remembered who his people were, and he remembered who God is and what He'd promised.

Caleb actively remembered for forty-five years! He rehearsed what was required of God's covenant people—a decidedly theological notion! He remembered that he was part of a plan, a dream, and a family with a future. And though others around him had lost sight of it amidst the ravages of the wilderness and the battles with enemies, Caleb's memory never wavered.

Because he knew *where he'd come from,* he understood precisely *where he was.* As a result, he also knew exactly *where he was going.* Caleb didn't draw his bearings from the fog around him; he was anchored in history!

Remembering is the foundation for everything. We're *anchored* by remembering history. Take a few minutes' break here and read your way through a psalm of remembrance or two. Psalm 136 is one such psalm. Watch God's people exercise their memory. Watch them rehearse what God has done. And then reflect on the amazing miracle of how such remembrance has strengthened the Jewish people through the centuries. They are the only people ever scattered in other cultures across the globe for a couple thousand years who have still managed to maintain a collective identity. And after twenty centuries they've managed to restore their own national entity. God is not finished with them yet. A "settled memory" matters—personally, familially, nationally, and spiritually.

A settled memory is like an anchor to the warrior soul. Although I've never been in the navy, I do understand a couple of basics—such as an anchor.

Have you ever seen an aircraft carrier? Multiple stories high. A flight deck measured in acres. A crew of thousands. The thing is a floating city. And it's the most powerful destructive force in the world, carrying guns, planes, and tons of armaments. But even for all its sophistication, it can never forget the basics—such as an anchor. In fact, it has two anchors. For what purpose? To keep that big ship from drifting! The most advanced weapons technology in the world can't get away from an anchor. If a carrier at anchor ever drifts through a harbor, believe me, you don't want to be in the way.

An anchor is meant for one thing—to hold steady. And that's the role of a settled memory in the soul of the warrior.

Ask any GI on a land navigation course: if you don't know where you've come from, you'll have a tough time knowing where you are, let alone where you're headed. It's called disorientation, being flat-out lost. If you've ever been there, you know its panic-striking horrors.

It is critical for a warrior to be grounded in history...to have a settled memory.

A settled memory—reminders and remembering—can restore hope, fortify faith, lift from discouragement, warn of traps and snares, turn us from destructive directions, keep us from wasted potential, and pass on life-enriching truths to others around us. We need reminders that speak to us of who we really are, what God has done for us, what our ultimate destinies will be, and how we should act in the meantime as believing warriors on planet Earth.

History Matters

Remembering is one of the most critical of warrior skills—owning a sense of heritage, history, belonging, and identity with those who've gone before. That's why tradition is so important to the military community. Unit history; casing the colors; battle streamers—it's all part of the warrior community. Never, never, never forget.

General Peter Pace served as commandant of the Marine Corps and chairman of the Joint Chiefs of Staff. He was the single most powerful man in an American military uniform. And every morning at the Pentagon, when he sat down at his desk to face the far-reaching decisions of the day, he stared straight into a photo he'd placed under the glass on his desk.

The face in that photo was of the young marine who was the first to die under Pace's command as a platoon leader in Vietnam. The general was determined to remember where he'd come from, where he was today, and whom he was serving in his every deliberation.

Peter Pace is a wise man. I was in a room with him only once, but I would follow the man down any alley anywhere on the globe. He's a leader who refuses to forget.

Every mature warrior develops a disciplined faithfulness to respect the past, remember healthy roots, and recommit to the fundamentals such as founding statements, documents, and principles. He guards against historical dementia—a disease that eats at the heart of every person and every people. Unless treated seriously, it will eventually kill you.

As spiritual warriors, you and I *must* remember. How many Christian lives are shipwrecked because an individual in a weak season of spiritual dementia *forgot* who he was in Christ and fell hard into sin? The carnage is severe—individuals, marriages, families, and churches are left wounded deeply and often limping for the rest of their lives. Develop the habit and skill of disciplined remembering!

When was the last time you read a good a history book of any kind? Maybe you're not into "macrohistory." But all of history consists of only a few basics—people and stories, events and stories, and ideas and stories.

Start with people and stories. Again, can you make a habit of reading quality biographies—both spiritual and national? Remember, as a soldier you're standing on some pretty broad shoulders today. How well do you know those shoulders? Washington, Henry Knox, John Adams and his cousin Sam from the Revolutionary War days. Andrew Jackson from the War of 1812, and Stonewall Jackson from the Civil War, along with Lee and Grant, Armistead and Chamberlain. Roosevelt at San Juan Hill, and Pershing in World War I. Then World War II's MacArthur, Marshall, Eisenhower, Patton, Bradley, and Gavin. Westmoreland and Abrams and Hal Moore from the Vietnam era. And after them, Franks, Petraeus, and McChrystal. Not to mention the thousands of citizen-soldiers who served under and beside them. Do you know the stories? They're available. *Read. Read. Read.* Readers are leaders.

And at the specific spiritual level, do you read Scripture and biographies of great Christians as spiritual history written for your personal growth? You and I desperately need the lessons of history and those "moral touchstones." *We must remember.* Every thoughtful remembrance becomes a piton below which we cannot fall. To remain free and healthy people, we must learn to drive a stake at the point of our values. To be effective believers, we must remember life's anchor points.

I'll never forget my own grandfather, after catching me cheating at a table game, looking into my seven-year-old eyes and saying, "Stu, you're a Weber boy. And Weber boys don't lie or cheat." That moment around that old yellow Formica table became an anchor, a settled memory, a stake driven into the rock for me. *I must remember. And the remembering will strengthen my walk.*

Every warrior needs a settled memory. Develop yours! Read and think.

✯ Chapter 7 ✯

A PERSONAL INTENSITY

One Man's Anxiety Is Another Man's Adrenaline

Everything can be taken from a man but one
thing: the last of the human freedoms—to choose
one's attitude in any given set of circumstances.[1]
• VIKTOR FRANKL •

WHO CAN FORGET the opening scene of Steven Spielberg's *Saving Private Ryan*? One word captures it: *Intense!*[2]
Every stomach in the theater was in knots. Every moviegoer's pulse was up. And that was just a movie depiction. Multiply that screenplay by real life, and you can only begin to imagine the sheer horrific intensity of D-Day 1944. The whole world was focused on what was happening on a few miles of beach on the northern coast of France.

If we multiply by several times the intensity on the screen for just the first half hour of *Saving Private Ryan*, we still have only a vague impression of just how intense combat can be. Yet people exited the theater absolutely exhausted, after 169 minutes of merely *watching*. And it was just a *movie*.

But D-Day on Normandy was much longer, more stomach-tightening, and more fearsome. And no one could call a time-out, take a break, or make a run for popcorn. There were no intermissions on Omaha Beach. No one could shut his eyes in an attempt to block out what was happening.

The off-the-chart risk factors and beyond-hyper intensity of actual combat is overwhelming, draining, and confusing.

INTENSE MEN FOR INTENSE BATTLE

Such battlefield intensity requires warriors and warrior-leaders of great personal determination. I'm speaking of individuals with a calm, a reserve, a steadiness, and an unrelenting intensity—people such as Lieutenant Colonel Hal Moore of *We Were Soldiers* fame. The man had to make decision after decision in the nerve-wracking chaos of battle, in the emotion-ripping environment surrounded by his own men wounded and dying. There's absolutely nothing on this earth that can compare to such intensity.

Every warrior soul must be intensely focused, completely undistracted, and powerfully driven. The warrior must be consumed by his calling. Eyes must narrow to focus. Brains must swell to absorb. And nothing is as it seems. The sheer intensity of warfare demands equally intense warriors to carry the day.

If intensity doesn't come naturally to you (it seldom does to most), find a fellow believer who exudes it and let it rub off on you. It will. Hang around him and let yourself catch some of his dust. I recall one younger Christian reluctantly signed up "just to tell the Bible story" at a summer 5-Day Club for children. In the process he had the privilege of leading youngsters to Christ. And he was never the same—hasn't slowed down yet. Twenty-five years later, as an elder in his church, he's still exuding that learned intensity, and it's still motivating others to swim along in the wake, like one goose in formation drafts behind the next, making it easier for everyone.

Intensity does not have to be loud. But it does have to be focused. It is not necessarily brash, but it is contagious. Intensity does not have to be talkative. But it is consistent. To my mind now comes a very specialized and much-needed ministry in our church. For want of a better term (good grief, it doesn't even have a logo or a poster), we call it simply "the wood ministry." In a slow economy where single moms need a lot of help and in a climate where cold winter requires a lot of fuel, a couple of guys headed up an effort to collect, cut, and deliver firewood to folks who needed it. It is now a mainstay ministry. There is a section of the church property covered with impressive stacks of cordwood ready to be distributed. And distribute it the guys do. The two guys who head it up are basically quiet, not particularly talkative, "preachy" guys. But they are respected and contagious. There you have it: a couple of quiet but consistent, unrelenting but servant-hearted, stand-up-and-get-to-it guys. And the body grows. And more than just hearts are warmed. Everybody wins.

On another scale there is Winston Churchill. He was a careful student of history who thought historically—which is another way of saying he recognized the big picture, the transcendent realities. By the time he was twenty-six, he'd finished his schooling, gone off to India, served with great distinction in the army, and become a decorated war hero. He was a member of Parliament and a gifted lecturer and author. Clearly Churchill was one focused, alert, absorbing, and determined individual.

Years later, when Britain was badly battered by the Nazi war machine early in World War II, the Brits named him prime minister. They knew collectively that only a man of undistracted intensity could lead the nation through its darkest days. When he stood before the House of Commons on June 4, 1940, he had to have a fire in his belly and steel in his eye. His remarks that day, delivered with an incredible personal intensity, so inspired individuals and the nation that Britain's darkest night would be turned toward her finest day:

> We shall not flag or fail. We shall go on to the end, we shall fight…we shall fight on the seas and oceans, we shall fight with growing confidence and growing strength in the air, we

shall defend our Island, whatever the cost may be, we shall fight on the beaches, we shall fight on the landing grounds, we shall fight in the fields and in the streets, we shall fight in the hills; we shall never surrender.[3]

There you have it—a man of great personal intensity. While others cowered, Churchill ran to the cause. That cause—a source of great anxiety for common men—was for Churchill a source of warrior adrenaline.

It takes a warrior soul to stand in the gap... to refuse excuses... to hold ground... to accept responsibility and lead others toward it.

What we're talking about here is a basic sense of *duty*. I once heard a preacher say we should always follow Christ out of love, not duty. I do not believe that. Love and duty are not antonyms; they are kissing cousins, if you will. They go together, as we say, hand in glove (you decide which is which). Follow the thread of "duty" here: To save the world, it took a Savior. To be a Savior, it took a Man. It took that Man, Jesus, to *stand* in the gap, to refuse His own personal wishes, to *hold* the *high ground* of Calvary, and to encourage His followers to take up their cross as well.

Think about it. Did Jesus *want* to go to Calvary? I expect not. He said as much, "Father, if there is *any* other way." (See Matthew 26:39.) I infer Christ's words to mean He would have preferred another way. But, like the magnificent Son-under-authority and warrior that He was, Jesus replied, "Nevertheless, Thy will be done." What motivated Jesus to do that? I believe it was a divine combination of both love and duty. Could Jesus's response be paraphrased as, "Yes, Father, as You command"? I think so.

So how about you? When was the last time you stood up, refused excuses, accepted responsibility, and stepped out to take the lead in some form of ministry? Try it. You might even find it life-changing. It has been life-changing for many of the people from our church body who swallowed hard and traveled to a third world country on a short-term mission trip. They may have signed up out of a sense of love and duty, but they came back with even more—a renewed spiritual, personal intensity like we'd never seen in them previously. And in the wake of their own spiritual soldiering, others took up the charge as well. Take some responsibility. Get intense.

Recently a young man from our church family entered the United States Military Academy as an eighteen-year-old plebe. One of his earliest lessons as a warrior-in-training was to learn to take responsibility. It's intentional at West Point. Within what seemed like only moments of arriving, he'd learned to accept responsibility. He was told there were only three acceptable responses to any of his leaders—"Yes, sir." "No, sir." Or, "I do not understand, sir." No excuses. No explanations. No blaming others. Only responsibility. West Point is in the business of building leaders of character—and intensity—for the good of the nation.

Intensity keeps you on target, on task, and functioning when others waver. And it moves others to join you. Yes, get intense. Take a risk. Sign up to teach sixth-grade boys. Don't leave it to others. No excuses. Get out there and soldier for the King.

For example, apply this same kind of intensity at your work every day. View your occupation as a duty station. After all, God put you where you are for His kingdom purposes. You are on the front lines of His mission. Apply your warrior soul. You may not need the kind of courage that dodges bullets. But you do need to exercise your warrior soul.

Most people could tell you what kind of character qualities make for excellent soldiers—things such as courage or bravery, loyalty and sacrifice, and a firm resolve to remain calm when the fires get hot. You need the same attributes in your duty station.

Are you calm and confident enough to maintain your focus when you are barraged with rapid-fire notices, requirements, and deadlines? Can you keep your cool?

Are you courageous enough to hold less than popular views in the workplace? Are you brave enough to appropriately challenge unethical practices or immoral behaviors? Are you strong enough to hold your own behavior in check under fire? Are you firm enough to refuse to surrender at the first sign of frontal challenge?

Living as a believing warrior in an unbelieving world that is clearly a battlefield is no easy task. Soldiers begin every day with a healthy dose of PT, or physical training. It's the basics—to stay in shape. Do you start your day every day with some serious "ST," or spiritual training, exercising your soul after God's thoughts?

It's your duty. And over time it will become your first love. Your character as a Christian warrior will be tested every day. Get used to it. No excuses. No blaming. Just old-fashioned soldiering. Your life may not be action-packed enough to make a great war movie, but I guarantee you, it's being recorded in the heavens. And one day you and your commander in chief, the King of heaven Himself, will have opportunity to review your game films. Stay strong, stay faithful, and stay in the fight. That's intensity. Let's look at some of it in an old warrior.

FOCUSED PURSUIT

Let's return to Caleb. This man had it. Remember again his phrase, so straightforward: "I followed the LORD my God fully" (Josh. 14:8). Check out that strong pair of words, *followed fully*. In Scripture, to follow less than fully is not to follow at all. The intensity of "following fully" so characterized Caleb's warrior life that the Spirit of God inserted that notable phrasing multiple times into the after-action report. Caleb used it of himself (in Joshua 14:8), as we've highlighted. Moses had used it of him too, as Caleb remembers in the following verse. And then we see it again in Joshua's assessment and reward of his comrade:

> So Joshua blessed him and gave Hebron to Caleb.... Therefore, Hebron became the inheritance of Caleb...because *he followed the LORD God of Israel fully.*
> —JOSHUA 14:13–14

These interesting words combine the twin qualities of following and focusing—so much so that they became a euphemism to describe the intense focus required of a hunter in pursuing his prey. Every twig out of place had to be noted. Every bent blade of grass had to be observed. Every twisted leaf was seen. Every bit of scraped bark was registered. Detail after detail after detail. *Focused following.*

Think of it as *focused pursuit.* I'm speaking here of focused pursuit of the mission; in other words, staying in the fight to the end and beyond, remaining undistracted, enduring, and ongoing. This is nothing less than an unrelentingly intense focus on the task and allowing yourself to be completely consumed by your calling.

It sounds a little like old Sam Whittemore, doesn't it? He was still trying to load his musket after a nearly mortal head wound and being bayoneted thirteen times. I sometimes smile and imagine that Sam descended somehow from Caleb's gene pool.

By this intensity, this being consumed by calling, the warrior soul sustains itself in battle.

My friend Gary Beikirch exemplified it at Dak Seang, a Special Forces A Camp only a dozen "klicks" (kilometers) from my location at Dak Pek. It was the same time of April 1970, the same siege, with the same two enemy regiments attacking. But Dak Seang was worse.

The camp medic, Gary sustained multiple debilitating wounds to his abdomen and lost the use of his legs because of damage to his spine. But he stayed at the task, pursuing his calling. In fact, he was so badly wounded that his teammates urged him to crawl back to the medical bunker and die. No dice. Not Gary. He had a deep personal intensity about him. The man was fully focused on pursuing his mission as team medic. He got his two assistants, teenage Montagnard tribesmen, to carry him to the fighting positions so that he, as the medic, could patch his teammates up sufficiently to keep them physically able to stay in the fight.

For his actions at Dak Seang, Gary was awarded the Medal of

Honor. He also holds the Distinguished Service Cross and the Silver Star for earlier actions. Being awarded the nation's three highest awards for valor is testimony to his intensity as a warrior. Gary survived, served many years as a middle school counselor, and is today an ordained minister of the gospel of Jesus Christ. (I tell his story in somewhat more detail in another book, *Infinite Impact*.)

Way to go, Gary! What an attitude—always living out the mission, even under the most adverse of circumstances.

You've likely heard of the shoe salesman sent by his manufacturer to a South Pacific island to sell shoes. Upon arrival he immediately demanded that the company return him home. "They don't even wear shoes down here," he exclaimed in frustration.

So the company sent a second salesman to the same location—same situation, same assignment. Upon arrival he immediately asked the company to ship him everything they had in inventory. His explanation? "They don't even wear shoes down here!"

One man's anxiety is another man's adrenaline. It's that same warrior spirit of personal intensity.

By sheer contrast I'm reminded of Winston Churchill's contemporary, Neville Chamberlain. In the face of Nazi demands Chamberlain caved, opted for appeasement. He didn't have the courage to stare injustice down. Fortunately for the world, where Chamberlain rolled over, Churchill stood tall. There was no "negotiating dialogue" with terrorists for him.

Thank God for Churchill, the greatest statesman-warrior of the most war-torn century in all of history. A world at war demands a leader of personal intensity and settled memory.

The military has another way of describing this quality of personal intensity, of focused following, of undistracted pursuit. Just two words: *mission first*.

The great apostle Paul evidenced a mission-first intensity numerous times. One occasion that stands out to me is his determination to visit Jerusalem one last time—to once again proclaim the truth of Christ there. He packed his bags for that journey, even though a number of his friends and colleagues—and the Lord Himself—warned him of the danger on that path.

The story unfolds beginning in chapter 19 in the New Testament Book of Acts. There we find Paul engaged in the demanding and eventful work of establishing a church in the city of Ephesus in Asia Minor. While there, "Paul purposed in the Spirit to go to Jerusalem" (Acts 19:21) after first crossing the Aegean Sea to take encouragement to various other churches he'd started earlier in Greece.

Midway through the next chapter we find him circling back near Ephesus again, this time saying his farewells to the church's leaders. In the presence of these men he recalled certain things about his earlier ministry there, things that they were well aware of—his self-sacrificial spirit; how he'd served them "with tears and with trials...through the plots of the Jews" (Acts 20:19); and how, despite constant opposition, he "did not shrink from declaring" the whole truth and purpose of Christ, and doing so with boldness (Acts 20:20–21).

Then Paul let them in on some sobering news that God had revealed to him—how he faced even worse treatment ahead:

> And now, behold, bound by the Spirit, I am on my way to Jerusalem, not knowing what will happen to me there, except that the Holy Spirit solemnly testifies to me in every city, saying that *bonds and afflictions await me.*
>
> —ACTS 20:22–23

With that kind of reception waiting for him, a normal man simply wouldn't go. But Paul was not a normal man. He was a warrior—a Spirit warrior—and a man of intensity. He openly stated:

> I do not consider my life of any account as dear to myself, so that I may finish my course and the ministry which I received from the Lord Jesus, to testify solemnly of the gospel of the grace of God.
>
> —ACTS 20:24

The man was utterly determined, no matter the cost, to complete his mission!

As Paul drew ever closer to Jerusalem, we next find him dropping in on Christian brothers and sisters in the city of Caesarea. And here, emphatically and prophetically, he was again warned of the danger awaiting him. Everyone "began begging him not to go up to Jerusalem," but Paul stood firm, telling them, "I am ready not only to be bound, but even to die at Jerusalem for the name of the Lord Jesus" (Acts 21:12–13).

The emotional exchange here between Paul and his friends concludes this way: "And since he would not be persuaded, we fell silent, remarking, 'The will of the Lord be done!'" (v. 14).

Hearing those words, you can almost hear Paul respond in exasperation: "Well, *thank you* for finally recognizing who's in charge here! *God* is! Thanks for granting me permission to fulfill my calling. Good grief, my earthly life doesn't mean a twit to me when it comes to serving my Lord! I'll do *anything* for Him! *I intend to be fully consumed by my calling.*"

That's the personal intensity of the warrior soul.

Lion Slayer

Can you name the greatest warrior in the Old Testament?

David? Maybe.

Jonathan? Good choice.

Moses? Once he woke up to reality, the man was a superb warrior.

There are quite a few excellent candidates. But I have a personal favorite. He's one of the lesser known men in the Bible, but even that is something I like about him. He wasn't looking for headlines; he was one of what I call the "little people in a little place just doing what they should"—the kind of people God uses to change history, the kind of warrior that turns a battle.

There's an obscure and strange little verse tucked away in the Old

Testament. You may have to blow the dust off the Book of 1 Chronicles in order to find it:

> Benaiah…killed a lion inside a pit on a snowy day.
> —1 Chronicles 11:22

Benaiah was my hero's name. His name translates as "the LORD has built." After reading of his exploits in Scripture, I suspect his name was something of a double entendre. The man was spiritually fit and could pump major iron! I suspect he too must have been downstream from Caleb's gene pool. Yet most preachers, with an exception or two, don't seem to deal seriously with this passage. To my knowledge, his name has never appeared in any published work on systematic theology. His story here at first seems to have no direct bearing on any major biblical doctrine (other than the hand of Providence watching over him in battle, no small thing!).

His name is tucked away in a few chapters of Holy Scripture that are strangely and wonderfully significant in a way that perhaps better known passages cannot claim.

Take a little time and sit down to read through two chapters, the eleventh and twelfth of 1 Chronicles. Notice the listing of name after name after name—of common soldiers. Dirt soldiers. GIs. Privates, specialists, lance corporals, and a buck sergeant or two. Some of these guys were ranking leaders by the time they're mentioned in these chapters, but what they all have in common is their experience as battle-savvy infantrymen in the kind of Iron Age combat that rendered the lifespan of most participants *very* short!

And here's a question for you, Christian: Why do you think God spent so much Holy Spirit–inspired ink on what appears to be a simple listing of the names of GIs in the ranks? (In my day we might have called it a "First Sergeant's morning report.") Why would God do that?

I like to think it's because God, the author of Scripture, has a special place in His great heart for warriors and for their soldiering. After all, His Son, Jesus Christ, was a truly exceptional warrior who still bears the scars of battle wounds. And God Himself is proud to be portrayed as the Warrior of warriors in Exodus 15 (verses 3 and following).

Check out this list of names in 1 Chronicles 11–12. These were men of character, called here "mighty men of valor." These were soldiers who had tasted battle and been found worthy. They were men of values, courage, loyalty, honor, duty, integrity, and selfless service. These were guys who would readily stand in between their community of values—their nation—and anyone or anything that sought to harm it.

Here's their summary description:

> Mighty men of valor, men trained for war, who could handle shield and spear, and whose faces were like the faces of lions, and they were as swift as the gazelles on the mountains.
>
> —1 CHRONICLES 12:8

Here's the major point of these two great chapters in Scripture: *Right makes might.* And *not* "might makes right."

These are men who conduct themselves in the spirit of a single phrase, intentionally repeated in the passage: "according to the word of the LORD" (found in verse 10 of chapter 11, then strategically repeated in verse 23 of chapter 12).

These men reflected the sheer might of disciplined strength— righteous, personal intensity—in guarding and securing the values of their community, a community consistent with God's values "according to the word of the LORD." These are warriors, not brutes. These are soldiers, not (to quote Clausewitz) "a bunch of hired assassins walking around in gaudy clothes... disgrace to God and mankind."4

These are men who serve "the LORD of hosts" (1 Chron. 11:9). That's a decidedly military term, one that's used, among other things, as the title for the commander in chief of the armies of ancient Israel. The Lord of Hosts is none other than God Almighty Himself.

No, the Holy Spirit didn't have to include these soldiers' names in the Holy Bible. He didn't have to "waste the ink" to do so. But He did it because He *wanted* to. I believe He included these names to honor these soldiers who epitomized their profession—individual warriors who embodied the principles and values of mighty men of valor indeed.

GOD LOVES SOLDIERS
AND GOD LOVES *SOLDIERING*

Judging from His Word, God seems to think extremely highly of soldiers and soldiering. As we noted earlier, the vocabulary of war appears everywhere in Scripture. Do yourself a favor sometime: do a little Bible study. Here are a few passages to check out:

- *Genesis 3:15:* As we've noted, this first hint of the Messiah describes His future appearance as a wounded warrior—coming in a context of adversity and enmity and exchanging blows with the champion of evil. And though shedding His own blood (by being wounded on the heel), He deals the ultimate death blow to the evil one by striking him on the head.

- *Genesis 14:14–15, 18:* We touched on this one earlier as well. No less a biblical hero than Abraham ate a sacramental, worshipful meal of celebration after defeating his enemies with 318 armed and trained soldiers of his own household.

- *Exodus 15:* The "wonders" He has worked that are praised here are victorious military actions (vv. 1–3, 6–7, 10–12). Here God overtly calls Himself a warrior.

- *Exodus 17:8–13*: Moses, the great lawgiver himself, raises his staff to God to ensure Israel's military victory "with the edge of the sword."

And there's more. In Leviticus soldiers are recorded observing certain ceremonial worship requirements similar to those of the priests who served the tabernacle. In Joshua we see the attack on Jericho launched as God's people surround the city with an enormous worship service centered around the spiritual leaders, the priests, and the ark of the covenant.

In 1 Samuel Jonathan emerges as a great warrior. I often think that's what drew him to David in the first place. Here was a man with similar courage, a man who wouldn't run from battle but who faced enormous odds straight on. Read 1 Samuel 14:1–15, and you pretty much have to conclude that Jonathan was Ranger-qualified, as he executes Special Ops missions on the cliffs between Michmash and Geba.

David, the man after God's heart (1 Sam. 13:14, Acts 13:22)—a man who, according to the New Testament, "served the purpose of God in his own generation" (Acts 13:36)—was clearly marked as a warrior. He wrote the Soldier's Psalm, as Psalm 144 is often called, where he gives none other than God Himself all the credit for making him into a warrior in the first place:

> Blessed be the LORD, my rock, who trains my hands for war,
> and my fingers for battle.
> —PSALM 144:1

And, again, it's none other than God Himself who keeps him in the conflict and grants him victory:

> My fortress, my stronghold and my deliverer, my shield and
> He in whom I take refuge, who subdues my people under me.
> —PSALM 144:2

Even after all of that review of Scripture, I still have some friends who say, "Well, I appreciate those biblical notations—but of course, all those passages are in the *Old Testament.*"

True enough. I grant you that. But will you grant me that the Old Testament is no less the Word of God than the New? Will you agree with the scriptural statement that our God is "the same yesterday and today and forever" (Heb. 13:8)? That there is no "shadow of turning" with Him (James 1:17, KJV)?

But just for fun, let's take a glimpse into the New Testament:

- John is the guy known as the beloved apostle and the apostle of love. But in 1 John 3:8, under the inspiration of the Holy Spirit, this apostle (once known as a "Son of Thunder") uses some distinctly military terminology. Keep in mind that the infantry's mission is to "close with and destroy the enemy"; then read what John says to describe how Jesus would "close with" our planet in His incarnation: "The Son of God appeared for this purpose, to *destroy* the works of the devil."

- Jesus Himself had high praise for the soldiers He encountered during His public ministry. In fact, He "marveled" at the character of a rough-and-ready soldier in Matthew 8:5–10. Jesus stated bluntly how impressed He was with this warrior's faith; in fact, He indicated that no one's faith in all of Israel could match it. This centurion, a captain of Roman infantry (tough dude!), had responded to Christ in the context of his military training: "I am a man under authority," he explained. He was telling Jesus, in essence, "I'm a soldier. I understand authority. And I know moral authority when I see it. You just say the word, Sir, and it's as good as done!"

- Finally, some of the most potent (and violent) military language in all Scripture is reserved to describe Jesus's second coming to the planet (as we've seen already in Revelation 19:11–16). You might say that in His first coming, he came as a Lamb. But the second time He'll be the Lion of Judah coming to take total control of His kingdom. While the Messiah in Genesis was prefigured as a wounded warrior, the Bible's final description of Jesus is that of a victorious warrior mounted on a great white war horse, armed for battle, launching the only true war to end all wars at the end of time. We can legitimately say that Jesus Himself is, first and last, a warrior.

Please understand that there's no disconnect whatsoever between the Testaments. The God of the Old Testament is the God of the New. When you read thoughtfully through the Bible, from Genesis to Revelation, you'll find an impressive consistency in the gradually unfolding story, in history, of God's victory over sin, over evil, over nations, and over death. One biblical scholar sums it up succinctly, writing that God will have victory in and over history "through mighty acts of justice—that [are] again and again, acts of retributive judgment. Goodness and severity go together in this story.... From Genesis to Revelation, God's character remains consistent. He is a loving, powerful, holy judge—and warrior against evil—from beginning to end."[5]

Yes, the Bible contains stories of one bloody battle after another. Sometimes Christians—and others as well—are seriously troubled by the fact that God seems to be at the center of so many battles and so much violence. People object to Christians being involved in war by asking how this can possibly square with Jesus's own words to His disciples, "I say to you, love your enemies" (Matt. 5:44). But confusion accumulates around those instructions when we fail to see they are Jesus's words to His followers as *individuals*.

This is, of course, the subject of another book or series of books. Let me just sum it up quickly here. The individual Christian ethic of love toward individuals (in Matthew 5–7, for example, the Sermon on the Mount) does not in any way contradict the national ethic of protecting the community of values (the nation) in a just war under properly constituted civil authority (Rom. 13:1–7)—which, of course, falls within the purview of God's sovereign freedom to judge nations and peoples. Lt. General Boykin will deal more with this issue in an upcoming chapter.

Here's the undeniable point. In the economy of God, soldiers have been and will be much used by God to further His own plans. (In fact, the apostle Paul actually took a *fourth* missionary journey at government expense and escorted by Roman soldiers as bodyguards! OK, it was a journey to trial, but the warrior in Paul was never one to waste an opportunity.) The point is indisputable—throughout all of history God has used wars and soldiers in life's chess game. He has used war and warriors both to judge as well as pursue people and nations. And He'll continue to do so until the end of time, when He comes again to take over and eradicate all rebellion against Him.

You and I and every honest reader of Scripture must note that *God loves soldiers!* I believe He has a special place for them in His great heart. I hope you do too.

And our friend Benaiah must have as special a place as any.

INTO THE PIT

Let's look closer at this guy, as we return to 1 Chronicles 11 and 12, where Benaiah is prominent.

Benaiah's feats in battle were remarkable enough—enormous feats of strength and agility on the battlefield so outstanding that he was eventually elevated to serve as the chief of security among King David's personal palace guards. Fiercely loyal to David, he would eventually serve his king as the chief of staff of Israel's military forces. But while he was still a rough-and-ready dirt soldier, we get a glimpse of him in that one tiny (and curious) verse tucked away in Scripture that has fascinated me for years.

Here's that verse again, this time in full:

> Benaiah the son of Jehoiada, the son of a valiant man of Kabzeel, mighty in deeds, struck down the two sons of Ariel of Moab. He also went down and killed a lion inside a pit on a snowy day.
>
> —1 CHRONICLES 11:22

He went down and killed a lion in a pit on a snowy day. Fascinating! Whatever would prompt such an act? What in the world motivated the man to face off with a lion, especially a trapped one? Was it a barracks dare? Was it just another "challenge" of the kind often tossed around in soldierly braggadocio? Or was it connected somehow with "post security"? Was the lion harassing an encampment? Was a trap laid for him (a trap that worked!)? Was it a matter of, "Now what in the world do we do with him?"—and Benaiah drew the short straw? Did some frustrated senior officer order his best man, "Get down there and take care of that thing. I don't care how. I just want it done—*now!*" If you've been a soldier long at all, chances are good you've heard frustrated "salute and execute" orders like that.

Honestly, I have no idea how or why Benaiah was in that pit. But I do know the story is in the biblical text. And I know it's there for a reason. So what can we learn from this tiny little verse? What can we learn about life, about soldiering, about faithfulness?

For my part, I think it offers us a lesson in soldierly character and conduct. Make that just plain Christian character. Perhaps the single greatest quality of a warrior is *endurance.* That never-say-die, one-foot-in-front-of-the-other, never-surrender, never-quit attitude that just keeps on keeping on.

Endurance, and the ability to perform under enormous pressure, is pretty much the major point of the US Army's Ranger School.

More than that, endurance is in fact a spiritual quality highly valued by Scripture. It's viewed as a critical element. Whether it's soldiering, life in general, or spiritual life in particular, endurance is an absolutely critical element.

Biblically, *endurance* can be defined, quite literally, as "remaining under." And the Christian is instructed and commanded to allow endurance to bring about its maturing effect—"Let endurance have its perfect result, so that you may be perfect and complete, lacking in nothing" (James 1:4).

Let's think about Benaiah for a moment here. The guy is...

> *...in a pit*
>> *...with a lion!*
>>> *...on a snowy day.*

Sounds like a Ranger School project to me.

- *"In a pit"*—that means, at the very least, a confined space with no exit. It was do or die.

- *"With a lion"*—that means it was critically hazardous duty. And remember this is around 1000 BC. There was no health administration overseeing workplace hazards or congressional committees assigned to study "risk aversion." There was just one exceptional Iron Age warrior having a go at it.

- *"On a snowy day"*—that means adverse circumstances. Sounds more like Ranger School all the time, at least if you were a "winter Ranger." Did you know the temperature can drop well below freezing in the Florida panhandle, and that it can snow there? I witnessed it firsthand. We "bony Rangers" nearly froze to death (some actually have—to the great regret and loss of career for some cadre[6]).

To all the above, add the likelihood that any cat in a trap is likely both mad and hungry. And the day is cold and slippery.

The odds aren't good for Benaiah.

Sooo…how's it going down there, Benaiah? Can you visualize his fire-team buddies hooting from the safety of the ground level above?

We don't know all that happened, but we know this: at the end of the day, when the snow had cleared, Benaiah was alive and the lion was not! To use military lingo in summing it up: "Mission first!"

Like Benaiah, soldiers, including spiritual warriors like you, just get the job done, whatever the circumstances, whatever the odds, whatever the risks. Salute and execute. Do the right thing. Just do it. Do the difficult thing. Take it and get it done. Stay in the fight, no matter what. Remember, believer, it's your duty.

Benaiah endured through his task, and that's not only a godly trait, but it's also the warrior soul.

READY TO ENDURE

Perhaps the most fundamental of all soldier skills is the ability to endure…to remain under…to put the mission first. And that requires some personal intensity.

That's the way a good soldier thinks. Good soldiers learn quickly that their lives aren't about themselves. The cemeteries of our land, and many others, are filled with the bodies of young soldiers who were willing to cut short their own lives that others might live full lives in temporal freedom. In the words of Jesus Christ Himself, "there is no greater love" than that.

As for me and my house, we thank God all the time for such soldiers—intensely sacrificial warriors who put themselves in harm's way for the sake of others.

Here's the US Army's Soldier's Creed. Think on these things:

> I am an American Soldier.
> I am a warrior and a member of a team.

I serve the people of the United States and live the Army
Values.
I will always place the mission first.
I will never accept defeat.
I will never quit.
I will never leave a fallen comrade.
I am disciplined, physically and mentally tough, trained and
proficient in my warrior tasks and drills.
I always maintain my arms, my equipment and myself.
I am an expert and I am a professional.
I stand ready to deploy, engage, and destroy, the enemies of
the United States of America in close combat.
I am a guardian of freedom and the American way of life.
I am an American Soldier.[7]

That is some personal intensity!

So how do you see your own spiritual intensity in this dark world? Have you bothered to develop a personal creed or statement of your warrior values? Do you rehearse a set of spiritual values regularly? It may be good to develop your own personal spiritual warrior creed or statement and rehearse it regularly. Recall this well-known example. It is attributed to a young Rwandan man faced with impending martyrdom—either renounce Christ or die. Reportedly, before his execution, he wrote this description of his own faith-building personal intensity: it is marked by a personal battlefield intensity.

> I'm part of the fellowship of the unashamed, the die has been cast, I have stepped over the line, the decision has been made—I'm a disciple of Jesus Christ. I won't look back, let up, slow down, back away or be still.
>
> My past is redeemed, my present makes sense, my future is secure. I'm finished and done with low living, sight walking, smooth knees, colorless dreams, tamed vision, worldly talking, cheap giving & dwarfed goals.

My face is set, my gait is fast, my goal is heaven, my road is narrow, my way is rough, my companions are few, my guide is reliable, my mission is clear. I won't give up, shut up, let up until I have stayed up, stored up, prayed up for the cause of Jesus Christ.

I must go till He comes, give till I drop, preach till everyone knows, work till He stops me & when He comes for His own, He will have no trouble recognizing me because my banner will have been clear.[8]

Sounds a lot like Caleb to me! I imagine the two of them will have some rollicking stories to share with each other around heaven's campfires.

Chapter 8

AN UNFLAGGING OPTIMISM

The Warrior's Quiet, Professional Confidence

Praise the Lord, and pass the ammunition![1]
• CHAPLAIN HOWELL FORGY •
USS *NEW ORLEANS,*
PEARL HARBOR, DECEMBER 7, 1941

YOU'VE HEARD OF "the zone." It's an observable human phenomenon when, for example, an athlete hits full stride. When he's "in the zone," he can't miss the jump shot, he catches an over-the-shoulder pass in full stride, and his curveball moves like a boomerang.

When a guy's in the zone, he simply takes over the game. Opponents can call a time-out, switch defenses, change the pace, adopt a fresh strategy, but it doesn't much matter. Being in the zone changes everything.

In the zone is where every warrior is at his best. But it's not always easy to stay there.

They say only two things can knock a guy out of the zone: *fear* and *anger.* (I think you could add a few more to the list—discouragement, depression, confusion, to name a few. But for now, let's stick to what "they" say.) Two little words—*fear* and *anger*—with one huge impact.

We're talking about *excessive* fear and *excessive* anger. It makes sense. When we're overly fearful or angry, we take ourselves right out of the game. Fear and anger blur our vision, rob us of our potential, and sap our strength.

I believe there's an antidote for fear and anger. The antidote is also packaged in two words. From my perspective they always run in tandem—*optimism* and *confidence*.

Bring It On!

Two words, different but related. Like first cousins perhaps.

Optimism.

Confidence.

And they work together like two guys in the army's annual Best Ranger competition. When one's down, the other lifts him up.

We've all heard the platitudes: optimists make lemonade out of lemons; optimists see the glass half-full when it's half-empty. Blah, blah, blah. Well, let me tell you: there's something to it. They're platitudes—trite, with nothing original in them—only because they're so incredibly common. And they're so common because everybody knows they carry some truth.

For my part I'd rather spend time with optimists than with their opposites. *Pessimists*—the word kind of sticks to your tongue. *Yech!* Who wants to be hanging around with a bunch of depressed victims and whiners? As a pastor who's worked with lots of genuinely depressed folks, and having experienced some depression myself, I can tell you the woe-is-me approach to life never worked well for anybody. Especially in a battle. Especially when it's a matter of life and death.

That's why I'm so drawn to men like "Uncle Sam" Whittemore. Half a face, thirteen bayonet wounds, knocked flat on the ground, left for dead—and the guy's still working at reloading for one more shot. I guess that's why I love the guy who throws a pass on fourth and long.

And that was Caleb. Like Sam, he's in his eighties and still going for it. Take note, some of my senior Christian friends. Your latter years are not for "retirement" to the golf course; those years are opportunities to be stewarded! Caleb got that.

In fact, he asks the CINC (commander in chief), Joshua, to give him the toughest assignment—"the hill country." In the language of the old King James Version, Caleb said, "Now therefore *give me this mountain*" (Josh. 14:12).

The terrain was rugged, even for infantry, but that didn't faze the old warrior for one moment. And he also wanted to lay claim to the most difficult objectives in that rugged terrain, "the fortified cities."

But Caleb wasn't done yet. He was itching to face down the worst, most feared enemies in the land—the Anakim. These sons of Anak were notorious warriors and genetically larger than normal men. They were also fierce and fearsome, and everyone in that part of the world knew it. Squaring off against an army of Anakim would have been every soldier's most ghastly nightmare.

But Caleb said, "Bring 'em on."

This eighty-five-year-old warrior, proudly wearing his old medals on his tunic, wasn't deterred by the mountain terrain, the fortified cities, or the oversized Neanderthals in body armor.

Man, I love Caleb! He was optimistic and confident even in the face of the seemingly impossible. Risk-averse? Not on your life!

And there are such men with us today. Thank God for them. I'm quite confident that same God wants you to be one of them. Are you strong enough to stand against unethical or immoral behavior where you work? Or are you spiritually risk-averse? Start to think more positively about God's intention to use *you* for His glory—every day.

Send Me!

Inside what is likely the US Army's most secure compound resides America's secretive counter-terrorist unit known variously as Special

Forces Operational Detachment 1, Delta Force, or simply "the unit." At the center of the compound stands the unit's Memorial Courtyard. Unlike most American memorials, this one is closed to the public. It's even difficult for a US congressman to gain access to it. This very private memorial is visited only by members of the unit. On limited occasions carefully cleared guests may be allowed a few moments there.

Surrounded by the unit's headquarters buildings, the courtyard is open to the sky. It centers around a high black granite wall on which are inscribed the names of unit members who have given their lives in service to our country. At the top of the wall, above the names, are chiseled these words from the Bible: *"Whom shall I send and who will go for us? Then said I, 'Here am I, send me!'"* Those words (from Isaiah 6:8) occupy the place of highest honor and respect in the compound; they also represent the attitude of the warriors selected to serve in the unit.

The unit's warriors are all volunteers. They've volunteered many times—not only to serve in our nation's army, but virtually all of them also volunteered for multiple other warrior-developing training: Ranger School, Special Forces training, the HALO course (high altitude, low opening parachuting), scuba training, a specialized sniper course, demolitions—the list goes on and on. These soldiers volunteer again and again for the most harrowing missions known to our military.

What makes anyone, even a soldier, volunteer to take such life-threatening risks? Some volunteers are undoubtedly motivated by personal bravado or some other ego need. But for the best of the best, there's a deeper recognition that *someone has to do it*, for much larger reasons. Every crisis demands that warriors possess not only a sense of transcendent cause, a settled memory, and a personal intensity, but also a humble yet disciplined confidence. It's a confidence that moves them to raise their hand.

Such a humble yet disciplined confidence, I think, is the same that we come to see in Isaiah after his encounter with the living

God. He said, "Here am I, send me." He was ready to engage. So it should be with believing warriors—to fight their own personal battles, yes, but even more, to step up to the larger calling of serving as kingdom warriors in the broader front of spiritual warfare across the planet.

HE THAT STANDS

It's a confidence reflected in the words of one our nation's Founding Fathers, Samuel Adams. After the Declaration of Independence was adopted, in a speech before Congress in Philadelphia, Adams stirred his fellow Americans with these words:

> If you love wealth better than liberty, the tranquility of servitude than the animated contest of freedom—go from us in peace. We ask not your counsels or arms. Crouch down and lick the hands which feed you. May your chains set lightly upon you, and may posterity forget that you were our countrymen.[2]

Clearly Sam Adams couldn't countenance those unwilling to raise their hands in national crisis. Later that year Adams's thoughts were echoed—with a plain-spoken power that etched the words in history—by another Founding Father. And never were such inspiring words more needed.

As winter came on late in 1776, George Washington and his Continental soldiers looked ready to collapse. They'd been defeated in New York, then staggered in a forced retreat across New Jersey and into Pennsylvania. But in the cold, dark days of December, Thomas Paine wrote a pamphlet he titled "An American Crisis," opening with these immortal lines:

> These are the times that try men's souls. The summer soldier and the sunshine patriot will, in the crisis, shrink from the service of his country; but he that stands...now, deserves the love and thanks of man and woman. Tyranny, like hell, is not

easily conquered, yet we have this consolation with us, that the harder the conflict, the more glorious the triumph.[3]

Washington had that pamphlet read aloud to his men in their secluded camp, and before the month was out, the commander and his Continentals—freshly inspired—had crossed the Delaware River and routed the enemy in a surprise attack at Trenton that sent shockwaves through the British Empire.

Yes, "he that stands now"—every single member of the US military—deserves our love and thanks.

And that was Caleb's attitude. Even at age eighty-five that old soldier wasn't sliding home or backing down. Caleb knew certain things; his transcendent cause was clear. He knew God, he had a grip on God's promises and covenants, and he believed that his Lord had a wonderfully large and transcendent cause for him to serve.

But Caleb did *not* know certain other things. He couldn't be sure how the battle would shake out, or whether he would survive. He didn't know if he would see Mrs. Caleb again, or ever have the privilege of sitting around the table with his children, or of hugging his grandkids.

The warrior knows there are no guarantees on the physical battlefield. And while we are assured of *ultimate* victory in the spiritual realm, there are no guarantees of specific outcomes in particular spiritual battles in this temporal world. For example, your attempts to "rescue" a sinning fellow believer from his sinfulness are not guaranteed to be effective. But the point is, you still "raise your hand" and engage. And you do it optimistically. "Perhaps" the Lord will grant a victory.

So—not knowing the future, but knowing the God who holds the future—Caleb raised his hand one more time. The man just never quit volunteering. Visualize his face if you can, as he says, simply and without pretense, "Perhaps the Lord will be with me, and I shall drive them out…"

That "perhaps" is a recognition of reality. Close combat always experiences close calls. I have one friend who cherishes a .45-caliber magazine that stopped a bullet that would have shredded his leg. The deep bruise quickly faded and was quickly forgotten. Most combat vets understand a firefight is a proverbial game of inches.

For the believer life is never a game of inches and has nothing to do with luck. A believer trusts his life to the hand of God and moves forward to fulfill his duty, understanding that nothing in this life—except God Himself—is certain. As David once expressed it, "I trust in you, LORD; I say, 'You are my God.' My times are in your hands" (Ps. 31:14–15, NIV).

With unflagging optimism firmly in place, Caleb actually seems to relish the coming challenge. For believing men like Caleb, "perhaps" voices more eagerness than hesitancy.

Caleb lived thirty-five centuries before Winston Churchill, but the Brit often captured the same spirit in his speeches, including these words in a brief address to schoolboys in 1941:

> Never give in, never give in, never, never, never, never—in nothing, great or small, large or petty—never give in except to convictions of honor and good sense. Never yield to force; never yield to the apparently overwhelming might of the enemy.[4]

Like Churchill, Caleb is confident. But notice that Caleb is not cocky. His words exude confidence in the Lord he knows personally and unflagging optimism. Caleb understands that his own future is in God's hands. And without presuming upon Him, he will depend upon Him and take whatever his Lord, in His providence, gives him.

BE MEN, BE STRONG

Biblical faith is like that: it follows the intentions of God's Word but never dictates the script. No one ever said it would be easy or fair.

But God did indeed say to His own, "I will be with you." (See Deuteronomy 31:6; Matthew 28:20; Hebrews 13:5.) Knowing that God would be with him was enough for Caleb, and it should be enough for any son or daughter of the living God.

Caleb exemplified the New Testament instruction to us: "Be on the alert, stand firm in the faith, act like men, be strong" (1 Cor. 16:13). Contrast that posture with that of most folks facing adversity: spirits drop, attitudes go south, and complaining sets in.

Jim McGuiggan, an Irish preacher, speaks to this:

> It would appear that some people just insist on being on the whining side rather than the winning side. Every time they open their mouths, it's a bleating session. You'd think the Bible had said, "Blessed are the moaners."[5]

But he reminds us of a great contrast:

> In every city in the world, in every age, you come across or read about people who have looked suffering right in the eye and refused to buckle under.[6]

That was more like Caleb. For him, it was simply a decision, a matter of choosing. Would he give place to faith in God or to frustration in the circumstances? And that made all the difference.

Chuck Swindoll tells the story of the fire that destroyed the laboratory and research files of Thomas Edison. Rather than mope and complain, or even sit down in shock while everything was going up in flames before his eyes, Edison hollered to his son, "Go get your mother; she'll never see another fire like this!"[7]

I'm thinking of an older pastor from my past who developed a serious form of cancer and was in the process of dying. The longer it went on, the worse his attitude became. His spirit just kind of folded up inside him, and he became something of a whimperer.

Then Mama came to town. His own mother, now very aged, sat

at his bedside and said, "Son, you've been teaching people how to live all your life. Now teach them how to die in your death."

Wow. That was a mother saying to a dying son, "Buck up, son. This is the last round. Win it!" If it came right down to it, I'd rather walk through a dark alley with that mother than with her son.

In a similar vein, McGuiggan passes along this story:

> A friend of U.S. Senate chaplain Lloyd Ogilvie had lost all vitality and enthusiasm and had become boringly negative. Ogilvie confronted him about it and assured him that now he had a choice between degenerating into the grave or living. Weeks later he received a letter of six words: "Dear Lloyd, I've decided to live!"[8]

Onward to Courage

The warrior skill of courage is something that flows out of a confident optimism. Like big John Wayne said, "Courage is being scared to death and saddlin' up anyway!"[9] That's the stuff. *OK, here's our situation. It ain't pretty, but it's ours. Let's do something about it.*

Psychologists spend a lot of time studying "luck." They recognize that optimists are simply happier, more well-adjusted people. So they counsel us to "see serendipity everywhere" and be sure to "prime yourself for chance."

Well, this world isn't such a sweet and happy place to see serendipity everywhere. And I for one have no intention of walking around talking to myself about getting primed for chance. But now that I "see," I'm more than willing to bow my knee to the all-knowing, everywhere-present, and omnipotent God of the Bible.

When good things happen in my life way beyond anything I can manufacture as a finite human being, there's more than enough time to look up and thank God, whose providential hand is involved in all of life.

Ask Joshua Chamberlain, commander of the Twentieth Maine at Gettysburg. It wasn't pretty for him, holding the end of the line, exposed on the flank, and running out of precious ammunition. I don't expect he was looking for serendipity around some tree trunk during those early July days of 1863. He was looking elsewhere. In fact, Chamberlain's life story, a magnificent biography, is titled *In the Hands of Providence*. (Buy the book and read it. It'll make a warrior out of you.)

Chamberlain—loaded with a sense of transcendent cause, a settled memory, and a slow-burning personal intensity—seized an opportunity. That's it. That's what unflagging optimism does. It's not foolish, but it does see the opportunity in a situation that makes the next guy just passively roll over. I believe it turns the tide more often than not, just as it did during the Civil War at Little Round Top.

Recall Stonewall Jackson and his words about feeling "as safe in battle as in bed." Surrounded by gun smoke, cannonballs, and raining debris, with all hell breaking loose around him, this man carried on with a warrior's quiet, professional optimism. Jackson would go on to state:

> God has fixed the time of my death. I do not concern myself about that, but to be always ready, no matter when it may overtake me.... That is the way all men should live, and then all would be equally brave.[10]

George Washington wasn't much different. Multiple times he was untouched in combat that no man should have survived. In one encounter he was the only officer unwounded, though he'd had two horses shot out from under him and four bullet holes left in his clothing. He was twenty-three at the time and had already survived a freak fire, smallpox, multiple Indian ambushes, fights with the French, and a near drowning. His personal after-action report, written to his brother, summed it up this way: "I now exist and appear in the land of the living by the miraculous care of Providence, that protected me beyond all human expectation."[11]

Both he and Stonewall knew the same God, Jesus Christ, the greatest warrior who ever lived.

The confident, professional optimism of soldiers such as Washington and Jackson is drawn only from the ultimate transcendent cause, God Himself. Our first president as well as old Stonewall would both swear to it—they believed, as do I, that our lives are lived under the sovereign grace of almighty God. And those who actually live their daily lives with that ultimate sense of transcendent cause—God Himself—exude a confidence that settles deep in their chests. They know this belief doesn't make them invincible, and though they wrestle with the same fears as any man next to them, they do so from a godly perspective. They do indeed make healthy warriors on a battlefield.

Those who do not know Christ, having witnessed the unpredictable "chance" evident everywhere on a battlefield—the near misses, close scrapes, shrapnel a razor's edge from an artery—are forced to relegate those realities to the inexplicable. So they reduce themselves to what is really a depressing perspective.

"Fate," they call it.

In other words, just crawl through life like some kind of worm that never knows when it's going to get stepped on.

Read this excellent, accurate, though somewhat discouraging description of a convoy in Iraq:

> "Incoming! Incoming!" came the recorded warning as the alert horn sounded. It was a sound that, by now, after so many such warnings, seemed less scary than melancholy, and the soldiers reacted to it with shrugs. Some standing in the open reflexively hit the dirt. The gunners who were standing in their turrets dropped down into their slings. But most did nothing, because the bullet had been fired, it was only a matter of time, and if they knew anything by now, it was that whatever happened in the next few seconds was the province of God, or luck, or whatever they believed in, rather than of them.[12]

Most did nothing. I get that. I've been there, and felt the same sensation and reactions. I judge no one for it. For a season I was one such numbed soldier. In fact, it was those kind of "if it comes in the hole with me now, there isn't a thing I can do about it" moments that began to change the course of my life. When the ground stopped shaking and the air cleared, I had to ask myself, "Now, why in the world am I alive when others aren't?" That question pushed me toward a spiritual pilgrimage that led me straight to the God of Washington and Jackson—and of thousands, even millions of other warriors like them.

An Open Mind

It's entirely possible that someone (perhaps you?) reading this book has not yet come to the very personal point of having chosen to become a believer in Jesus, If that's the case with you, are you willing to be open-minded about faith in Jesus Christ and His sovereign hand of Providence?

Having an open mind is important. Without it, we'll miss many opportunities. Ultimately, however, as G. K. Chesterton once said, "The object of opening the mind...is to close it again on something solid."[13] Facts are facts. Two plus two is four. Once we wrap our minds around solid reality, we're in a position to stretch beyond—because two plus two is four, we can begin to extrapolate the mathematics into the possibility of sending men to the moon. So it is with faith in spiritual realities.

If you'll open your mind to give Jesus half a look, you'll not be disappointed. He'll stand up to every test. He's full-on truth. And if you're truly open-minded, you'll have a good shot at seeing it for yourself.

Try it, with your eyes and your heart wide open, and see where it will take you. It will take you straight into a relationship with the Creator God, Jesus Christ, to whom our nation's founders looked in our national birth process. (If you're ready to take that challenge now, I suggest you flip ahead to the last chapter and meet, in a very personal way, this greatest warrior who ever lived.)

How's Your Trust Quotient?

Let's take a little closer look at ourselves, Christian warrior. Some of these "faith kinds of things" can appear to defy logic. They can tend to frustrate intellect, can't they? Consider this: It's not so much your intelligence quotient (IQ) that is at issue here. It's actually your trust quotient. So how is your "TQ"? Like David of old and Caleb of older, have you learned to spend more time expanding your TQ? David's world of physical combat was so intimately linked to his concept of spiritual warfare, he really didn't see much difference, if any. He breathed them together in the same sentence: "For by You I can run upon [translate that "crush"] a troop; and by my God I can leap over a wall" (Ps. 18:29).

David's TQ was so strong that he saw his worlds of physical combat and spiritual warfare as essentially one and the same. He didn't separate the two, didn't live in two worlds, didn't compartmentalize. For David, physical combat and spiritual warfare were two sides of the same coin. Perhaps that's part of the reason God so highly commended him in Psalm 78:72 for the "integrity of his heart." David's heart was not bifurcated. It was an integer, a single whole. How's your trust quotient? Leaving everything to a vague "fate" rather than an intelligent faith is a tough way to live.

Consider this combat episode from Iraq:

> Really, how else to explain…what happened to a captain named Al Walsh when a mortar hit outside of his door early one morning as he slept? In came a piece of shrapnel, moving so swiftly that before he could wake up and take cover, it had sliced through his wooden door, sliced through the metal frame of his bed…sliced through the rear of a metal cabinet…and finally was stopped by a concrete wall. And the only reason that Walsh wasn't sliced was that he happened

in that moment to be sleeping on his side rather than on his stomach or back, as he usually did, which meant that the shrapnel passed cleanly through the spot where his head usually rested, missing him by an inch. Dazed, ears ringing, unsure of what had just happened, and spotted with a little blood from being nicked by the exploding metal fragments of the ruined bed frame, he stumbled out to the smoking courtyard and said to another soldier, "Is anything sticking out of my head?" And the answer, thank whatever, was no.[14]

The answer, thank whatever, was no.

Most every combat veteran has had some kind of similar "What just happened?" experience. So what do we do with that? For the believer, the response is, "Thank You, Lord!"

Thank whatever? Many of the guys in Vietnam in my day— like many soldiers in many wars over many centuries, I expect— responded with a similar shrug. In fact, in my day, "whatever" wasn't an uncommon word to hear. It was usually heard along with a string of expletives and ending with something like, "_____, it don't matter." (OK, even the undisciplined grammar and enunciation was part of the numbed trancelike reaction.) *It don't matter?* Well, yes it does! It matters that I'm still breathing air and eating groceries. And it certainly matters to my fellow soldier who's no longer breathing. He's entered an eternity where he knows more about life and death than he ever did in this life.

So what do I do when I'm the one who's still breathing? What do I do with the life I've been "given back"?

I start looking for some answers, and I look in the right place: the Bible. That's where you'll find real-life encounters with the living God. And before long your trust quotient will rank right up there with the geniuses of faith, such as the three Hebrew children who went man to man with a tough king and fiery furnace: "Our God whom we serve is able to deliver us from the furnace of blazing fire; and...out of your hand....But even if He does not, let it be known…that we are not going to serve your gods" (Dan. 3:17–18). Whew, that kind of trust quotient will make a man out of you! Call it unflagging optimism.

TAKING THE MESS TO GOD

King David saw much more than his share of combat. He was also a thinker and always seemed to have room in his life for significant reflection. It may have started when he was just a boy, out in the backside of the wilderness with his daddy Jesse's sheep. Through long days and longer nights, this young man practiced the discipline of thinking about God—His Word and His ways. Yes, there were certainly times when he became depressed over the uncertainties and the inexplicable.

But here was David's secret: He didn't just stop there with another "whatever." He ran to God with his soul in his hands and searched His Word for an explanation. I love that about David, and I love that about his psalms.

On one occasion he was particularly wiped out. It had been a rough season, and circumstances had just about hit the bottom. On the run to save his skin from an insanely jealous king, he holed up in a cave with four hundred other survivors, none of them particularly positive about life, let alone ready for more combat:

> So David…escaped to the cave of Adullam.…Everyone who was in distress, and everyone who was in debt, and everyone who was discontented gathered to him; and he became captain over them.
>
> —1 SAMUEL 22:1–2

Talk about a depressing mess! *Esprit de corps?* Nonexistent! Not in that dark, damp, depressing cave amongst a bunch of discontents. We have a leadership issue here!

So what does David do? He does what he was learning to do more and more. He decides to take this mess before God, spreading out before Him on the ragged floor of that clammy cave. And he took notes!

His notes are recorded in Psalm 142. It's not a pretty psalm, but it's honest and open, right from the start:

> I cry aloud with my voice to the LORD; I make supplication with my voice to the LORD; I pour out my complaint before Him; I declare my trouble before Him.

David goes on to lay out his miserable circumstances (get out your Bible and read it): the enemy has laid traps for him; no one much respects or regards him; his only hope and refuge is God, his "portion in the land of the living"; he's "very low"; his enemy is too strong for him. (See verses 2–6.)

But you can see the light coming on for David. The realization that God knows his "path" begins to take root, so he prays to the only One who can help him and lift his soul in this dark depression. He begs God, "Bring my soul out of prison, so that I may give thanks to Your name" (v. 7).

What we've called the eyes of his heart are seeing more clearly. You can almost see the smile spreading again across his face, as he sees the day yet to come, a day of human comradeship under divine blessing: "The righteous will surround me, for You will deal bountifully with me" (v. 7).

Read through that psalm several times. Catch the spirit of it. And watch David begin to stop listening to his own soul and start preaching to it.

OVERWHELMED...BUT WAIT!

Let me show you what I mean. Look again at the verbs in the psalm. David is a mess. He's pouring it all out on the table before God.

The words *cry aloud* are strong ones; they describe a kind of almost involuntary guttural screech, the kind we sometimes make when in great pain.

Make supplication is David's way of saying, "I'm begging You, God. I'm at the end of my rope!"

Pour out is also a very strong verbiage. It means literally "to vomit." David is so wasted, he can't hold anything in; it's almost an involuntary gushing out of his soul.

And then there's a climax, right at the psalm's midpoint, in verse 3. In the original Hebrew there's actually an ellipsis, a break, a spot where David doesn't quite finish his thought. Instead, a realization— and a smile, so to speak—begins to spread through his soul. There's a focusing of the eyes of David's heart. After vomiting out the misery of his soul before God, a greater truth dawns on him.

Verse 3 can be translated like this: "When my spirit was completely overwhelmed within me...[there's the break]; but, wait— *You* know my path!"

The misery of the circumstances was totally overwhelming. He pours out his heart to God. And God's Holy Spirit pricks his soul to remember something critical: *God knows!* And He knows every detail, personally and intimately. Remember the old TV commercial where the guy drinks some sugary, worthless beverage, and then smacks himself alongside the head and says, "I could have had a V8!" In other words, "What was I thinking? I could have had something healthy!" That's the thought here. It suddenly dawns on David that there's a better, higher, brighter path for his thoughts than the rut in which he's been wallowing.

David's heart begins to rehearse what he comprehends about God. It's not unlike the refreshing of a settled memory. David remembers who he is, who God is, and who's in charge of even these miserable circumstances. David's memory settles on the personal nature of our God and His personal interest in every single one of us. This God isn't some distant clockmaker who created the world and wandered off in a fit of boredom. The God of the Bible is infinitely capable of relating to every detail of every one of our lives. All at the same time!

In my earlier skepticism I used to believe such thoughts were merely religious sentiment. I now know differently!

Hey, if IBM can hook a bunch of supercomputers together in a series sufficiently powerful to make hundreds of thousands of calculations per second (and they have, when the computer faced off with the world's king of chess, Garry Kasparov, in 1997),[15] then the Creator of the universe in His infinite omnicompetence is mind-blowingly capable of dealing with our lives. He even counts the hairs on your head (Luke 12:7). And that sounds like another foolish off-the-wall religious notion, until you know Him.

Drop back to Psalm 139, another of David's great psalms. Talk about mindblowers! In fact, that's precisely what David says in the first few verses:

> O LORD, You have searched me and You know me.
> You know when I sit down and when I rise up.
> You even understand my thought from afar.
> You actually scrutinize my path and my lying down.
> And You are intimately acquainted with all my ways.
> Even before there is a word on my tongue,
> Behold, O LORD, you know it all completely!
> You have enclosed me behind and before
> And laid Your hand on my shoulder.
> Such knowledge is too full of wonder for me;
> It is too high, too lofty; I cannot attain to it.[16]
>
> —PSALM 139:1–6

David, under the inspiration of the Spirit of God, is rehearsing the intimacy God desires and enjoys with each of His children. God knows everything, even the things we don't take the time to think about ourselves. He knows our every move. He actually has a path for each of us, and He scrutinizes (or "sifts") us so that we grow, so that the eyes of our heart see more clearly.

In verse 6 of this psalm David says all this is just too great to think comprehensively about it. In fact, he really can't grasp the wonder of it all. It blows all of his circuit breakers—*pop, pop, pop, pop.* It's "too high, too lofty."

I get that. How often I've felt as David did—"God, You're so incredibly wonderful, I can't get my brain around it all." True enough. If my pea brain could grasp the full reality of all that God is and does, He wouldn't be all that great. As it is, I'm simply left in awe of my Lord, of His love for me, and of His watch-care in my life.

Yes, I'm ever so humbly with Washington and Chamberlain "in the hand of Providence."

As an old soldier I particularly appreciate David's language in verse 5 of Psalm 139: "You have enclosed me behind and before." David, the warrior, is basically saying, "God, You walk point ahead of me; You have my back behind me, and You have my flanks on either side." David is verbalizing the reality that God Himself has you covered. God has the point, rear, and flank on every patrol that His children take on the path He's personally designed for them.

Push "fate" off the table. Push "whatever" off the table. Come to the living God! And walk every day of your life in His care.

Given that very personal path, given God's intimate knowledge of David and his ways, and given God's intimate involvement behind and before, David verbalizes in verses 7–12 that there's no place in all the universe he could go where God isn't there before and with him. Mountain summit or ocean depth, *God is there.*

The psalm comes to something of a climax in verse 16 where David, realizing God has personally formed him, says this:

> In Your book they were all written—
> The days that were ordained for me,
> When as yet there was not even one of them.

There you have it. Straight from the Word of God Himself. He determines when His children are called home. *I won't die one day before I'm scheduled to.*

Every human being will die; some will still be young, others will be old. But all die. As the child of a sovereign God, however, my death will come when *He* wants me home in heaven with Him. And not a second sooner.

That's why Stonewall Jackson told the young captain essentially this: "I don't sweat it, son. My faith teaches me that my life and my death are in God's good hands."

Stonewall was right. Such a faith would make all men brave.

HEALTHY DOSES OF OPTIMISM

Consider the unflagging optimism of some of the folks in the Bible. And recall, as you review their stories, that they hadn't read the end of their own story. It hadn't been written down in the Bible yet. When they took their optimistic actions, they had no knowledge of the future. They "only" knew God and His character.

Consider Joseph. The guy had all kinds of reasons to be depressed. Talk about ups and down, highs and lows. His life journey was full of bumps and bruises—deep, heartrending bruises and long-term bumps.

He went from being his father's favored son to his brothers' discarded garbage, tossed in a pit. He was *abandoned*.

He was left *alone and lonely*, carried off by a bunch of thugs involved in human trafficking, only to become a slave in a country he'd never seen, forced to learn a language he'd never heard. But then he gathered his wits and faith and worked his way up to an extremely responsible position working for the most powerful man in that country. The guy's wife propositioned him; Joseph refused the temptation. He was framed and tossed in an Egyptian prison. Again he gathered his wits and faith and was able to rise to a place of responsibility in the prison.

He helped out a fellow prisoner about to be released. The guy promised to remember Joseph to folks in high places after his release. But he forgot. For two more long years Joseph is in that prison. In all of this there's no record of a single word of complaint from Joseph. The guy refused to be a victim, refused to whimper. Many times the trajectory of his life seemed only downhill. Joseph just kept doing his daily prison chores, believing the promises of God.

Of course, you know the rest of the story. But Joseph didn't! Still, his humility, his disciplined confidence, and his unflagging optimism in God carried him throughout his life. Ultimately he finished on top, running all of Egypt, the world's superpower at the time. But for much of Joseph's journey, he had no clue of the outcome.

Throughout it all Joseph maintained a humble optimism and a quiet confidence in the purposes of the God he served. When it was all said and done, he summarized that long downhill stretch of his life with these words, spoken to his conniving brothers: "As for you, you meant evil against me, but God meant it for good in order to bring about this present result, to preserve many people alive" (Gen. 50:20).

Or consider the humble, disciplined optimism of Moses's mother in Exodus 2. This woman wove a tiny basket, waterproofed it as best she could, and put her infant son in it to drift on the river's current. And that little baby survived to become one of the most effective leaders in world history, and certainly one of the world's most famous individuals. Thanks, Mom, for taking faith-filled action in the face of hopeless circumstances! Way to be a warrior.

One of my favorite of such stories is that of Jonathan, prior to his knowing his best friend, David. Young Jonathan's godly confidence motivated him to launch a two-man special ops mission to penetrate the Philistine garrison. The entire Israeli army had degenerated into a state of depression in light of the sheer number of Philistine enemy facing them. King Saul, Prince Jonathan's father, was frozen by fear and indecision.

But Jonathan, like Caleb, knew God and His capacities.

So Jonathan and his armor bearer approached their enemy's

camp with a clear understanding of their lives being in God's hands: "Come, let us go over to the garrison of these uncircumcised. It may be that the LORD will work for us, for nothing can hinder the LORD from saving by many or by few" (1 Sam. 14:6, ESV).

We've heard that "perhaps the LORD" phraseology before, haven't we? Four hundred years after Caleb, Jonathan had learned the same lesson. No guarantees regarding the details. Only the promises of a faithful God: "I will be with you."

At the end of the day Jonathan and his armor bearer, only two warriors, had stood strong against ten-to-one odds, and twenty Philistines lay dead in the sand.

Unflagging optimism. It's the warrior's quiet, professional confidence.

A great story of unflagging optimism and soldierly confidence is told of one American GI on Christmas Eve 1944 in the Battle of the Bulge.

The Germans had shocked the world with a surprise forward attack that had broken the Allied lines. The Allies were in full flight. The Eighty-Second Airborne Division, in theater reserve, was ordered toward "The Bulge" with essentially a twofold mission: first, stop the fleeing Americans and get them turned around; and second, stop the oncoming German onslaught.

With the terrible winter weather prohibiting their flying and parachuting into place, the Eighty-Second humped the distance like battle-hardened foot soldiers. For days and nights, virtually sleepless, they moved. Arriving in the Ardennes, haggard and worn, they came upon the first elements of fleeing Americans.

One GI from the 82nd, extremely worn from the forced march, saw an American tank fleeing in his direction. He stood his ground in the middle of the small forest road. The tank stopped. With a cigarette drooping from his mouth, his darkened eyes in the back of their sockets, an M-1 hanging from one hand and a bazooka draped across the other shoulder, he asked the panic-stricken American tank commander, "You lookin' for a safe place?"

Of course he was.

The smoking trooper, like every warrior worth his optimistic confidence, added words to this effect: "Right here behind me is a safe place. We're the Eighty-Second. And this is where it all turns around!"

I think there may have been a couple expletives included in his actual statement, but you get the picture.

Unflagging optimism. Appropriate believing confidence.

Mission accomplished.

Chapter 9

A DEEP CAMARADERIE

Never Go Into Battle Alone; Leave No Man Behind

There is no substitute for the spiritual in war.
Miracles must be wrought if victories are to
be won, and to work miracles, men's hearts
must be afire with self-sacrificing love for each
other, for their units...and for their country.[1]
• MAJ. GEN. JOHN A. LEJEUNE, USMC •

I N 2008 I sat in the hot sun of Fort Bragg to witness the retirement from the army of a man I'm privileged to know as a good friend. (He even gave me a first-class, super-potent air rifle for my birthday...smile.) As I sweated through Bragg's humidity, I reflected on a lesson he'd punctuated for me.

He's one of America's most respected warriors, a soldier's general. At his retirement ceremony three dozen other general officers showed up to show their respect. Now that's unusual! People commented at the time it must have been some kind of record to have that many general officers present in one place, and for a retirement ceremony at that.

The guy was the consummate warrior—physically impressive (lifetime best bench press—507 pounds!), tactically fit (as a full colonel, he commanded America's most elite counterterrorist unit, Delta Force), and spiritually keen (with a personal thirst for God and an ability to discern the spirit and character of other men). Gary Harrell embodied all that is great about America's most valiant defenders. And he had the purple hearts to prove it.

Another unusual group was also present at his retirement. They were special guests who held a special place in Gary's life. The master of ceremonies formally welcomed "all the gun dealers and knife manufacturers present today." Yes, like any self-respecting warrior, Gary Harrell was intimately familiar with all the tools of his soldier's trade. He never forgot the basics. While he retired as a major general, well experienced in all the lofty "command and staff" functions every two-star general's career must necessarily include, Gary never lost sight of the fundamentals. He knew which weapons best fit the mission and circumstances. And he was never without at least one, more often several, somewhere on his body.

I asked him one day, "Gary, when you're going into combat— when you know you're going to see the elephant in the midst of a firefight—which weapon do you most want with you?" I'd anticipated him possibly mentioning his souped-up M4 assault rifle or his Kimber Ultra Carry .45-caliber handgun. But I wasn't prepared for his answer.

Without a second's hesitation, Gary's strong voice bellowed, "When I go into battle, I want a fellow warrior beside me who's big enough to carry me when I get hit!"

Gary grasped what's most important when the stakes are high and the chips are down—a friend. When the going gets toughest, every man needs a battle buddy. Every fighter pilot needs his wingman. Even the Lone Ranger was never alone. Tonto saved his skin many a time. And David, one of the greatest men, leaders, and warriors who ever lived, needed his Jonathan to "strengthen his hand in God" (1 Sam. 23:16).

Life is a battle. Earth is a war zone. And every one of us needs a Ranger buddy, a close friend or two, the kind of men to ride the river with us. It will make us better men, husbands, fathers, sons, friends, and soldiers.

Find a friend, my friend! Read on.

MADE FOR THIS

"You and me"—in those words from Joshua 14:6, I can hear the deep collegiality of the warrior fraternity echoing across the centuries. Joshua and Caleb had been soldiering together now for nearly half a century. That's a long time, long enough to know each other well. Long enough to see how a man responds under pressure. And plenty long enough for the cords of soul-knitting to have their effect. Over such time and under such pressure, mutual love and respect grow to uncanny levels.

I see that kind of love and respect for Joshua in those three little monosyllabic words that slip effortlessly, without need of fore-thought or calculation, from the lips of Caleb: "you and me."

Joshua 14:6 is a larger-than-life verse. Read it. Then go back and feel it.

The troops are bivouacked around Caleb and Joshua. The "sons of Judah" were those men who had faced combat together in the con-quest of Canaan. Many battles were behind them. The campaign had been long, hard, and successful. But it isn't over yet. There remains a handful of unconquered enemy strongholds. They're last remaining for a reason. They're formidable, the toughest objectives. Now it's time for the final push to complete victory. How shall these two old soldiers face a final campaign?

When I read the passage in Joshua 14, in my mind's eye I see men coming together to ready for the battle at hand. The battle council is gathered. The old soldiers are ready.

Caleb was forty when he and Joshua first ran recon together into the unknowns of Canaan. Time has passed. Battles have come and gone. Soldiers once, and young, they are soldiers still, and older. Age has seasoned them. But the fire is still in their eyes and hearts.

Joshua hears a well-known voice speak up. Can you hear the tone in Caleb's words? Can you see the respect in his eyes? Can you imagine the camaraderie these two enjoy? Can you visualize the spirit of the conversation between these two old veterans, battle buddies for decades?

You and me. You and me, old soldier. You and me, we still live for the God of Israel and His dreams. You and me, we still fight for His intentions. You and me, we can see the finish line. We're almost there, old buddy. You and me. One more time around. And hey, my brother, let's not hold back. Give me the roughest, toughest assignment. Let's do this. Together. *You and me!*

I believe Caleb's words are loaded with both wisdom and deep emotion. It's as though this mission is what he has lived for. Indeed, it is. He was made for this. And so were you! Soldiers were meant to stick together.

Karl Marlantes tells of such incredible "all for one, one for all" teamwork on the battlefield. His writing is consistently humble as he describes the heated moments for which he would receive the Navy Cross, the nation's second-highest medal for valor.

> Many of us coming up the hill saw Niemi [yet another member of the *unit*] sprint out into the open. Knowing now that he was still alive and that he and the chopper crew were dead for sure if we didn't break through to them, we all simply rushed forward to reach them before the NVA killed them. No one gave an order. *We*, the group, just rushed forward all at once. *We* couldn't be stopped. Just individuals among us were stopped. Many forever. But *we* couldn't be. This, too, is a form of transcendence. It was we, no longer me.[2]

Yes, indeed. Such awesome, soul-enriching *togetherness* is gloriously transcendent!

You may have witnessed it just as vividly in the spiritual realm as well. I have seen it repeatedly. How many times at a men's conference have we heard it said through an open microphone—"I couldn't have done this without my friend here beside me!"

The face of one such man comes to my mind just now. Successful in the world's eyes, he'd blown up more than one marriage. He hated his own sin that wounded himself and others so deeply. But everyone around him assumed him to be a self-sufficient type. He knew otherwise. Inside he was dying. Others figured he'd just move on. But he so hated himself, for the first time he was beginning to give up on himself.

Here's the point: even the apparently strongest and most self-sufficient among us need fellow warriors. Two guys came along for this guy. They stood beside him and opened their souls to one another. Over time their ongoing transparency and genuine love literally saved him from himself. Now he's doing the same for others—reaching out and hanging on to other guys in their despair, refusing to leave any man behind. Caleb's words have a ring to them, don't they—"You and me!"

PAGE ONE OF THE BIBLE

Yes, that is the profound reason for this kind of transcendent camaraderie. It's actually a part of the image of God in which we're created. Ultimately it is a reflection of the glory of the Creator in whose image we are made. Father, Son, and Spirit are inseparable. They are the triune God. All the value and joy of friendship that we experience is wonderfully downstream from the nature of the living God who created us.

Father, Son, and Spirit never act alone. They act, always and only, together. It is a mystery. And it constitutes the point of Genesis 22 and Abraham's faithful willingness to do the unthinkable and sacrifice his son. It's a prophetic type of Jesus and the Father attending the hill of sacrifice two thousand years later. The Genesis 22 passage reminds us repeatedly, "So the two of them walked on together." It's the Old Testament's way of picturing *the* Father and *the* Son, who would later walk up the same hill, facing the same sacrifice. But when Jesus and His Father climbed Calvary—and the two of them walked on together—there would be no substitute ram in the nearby bushes. Jesus was, indeed, *the lamb* who took away the sins of the world. Even in sacrifice, the Father and Son were together.

Together is better. It's part of the image of God, a plurality in unity.

Ever notice how Jesus commissioned His disciples? Jesus sent His guys out "two by two," as the Scriptures state it (Mark 6:7; Luke 10:1). Even the standout, indomitable Paul—though we often visualize him as a solitary, world-changing apostle—even he never traveled alone. If Timothy wasn't with him, Silas was. Or Luke. Or Epaproditus. Or Epaphras. Or...

Together is better. It's axiomatic. It's the image of God. You were made for it.

That axiom first appears on the Bible's page one: "It is not good for the man to be alone." While that verse in Genesis 2:18 is, of course, a direct reference to marriage—the original vessel to contain the glory of God—its broader implications are explicit everywhere else in Scripture. The human being is created in the image of God and was never intended to be alone.

Two of the Bible's greatest warriors epitomized that reality: "Now it came about...that the soul of Jonathan was knit to the soul of David" (1 Sam. 18:1).

Take some time out here. Open your Bible and read—slowly and reflectively—some of their exploits, beginning in 1 Samuel 14 and following chapters. These guys were battle-hardened Ranger buddies who faced ultimates—life and death—together. They had each other's back. They had each other's flanks. And they loved each other as competent, trustworthy fellow warriors. The power of friendship forged under adversity is one of life's greatest treasures.

Neil Roberts fell out of a helicopter. That's bad enough in itself, wouldn't you say? But Roberts landed in the snow on Afghanistan's Takur Gahr, an unforgiving behemoth of a mountain, ten thousand feet high. Worse yet, he landed in front of a bunker occupied by heavily armed Islamic *mujahideen*. The fireworks were fierce.

Malcolm MacPherson describes the impossible scene on "Roberts Ridge," and he captures the spirit of the US military's special operations community reflected in Neil's mind:

> His confidence stemmed from his life's experience, filtered through an inner, mysterious core. Surely one pillar, known to each man in special operations, propped up everything else: the knowledge that he would never be left behind in a fight, no matter what....
>
> In real war, the tradition was etched in the fifth paragraph of the Ranger Creed: "I will never leave a fallen comrade to fall into the hands of the enemy."...For special operators such as Roberts and those of the SEALs, SOAR, STS, DELTA, and Rangers, leaving a teammate in the lurch and not returning was far more serious than breaking any social vow...because it entailed death, and the dead man could easily be you. Returning for a lost brother required no thought, no decision. It was an ingrained reaction, not an idea.[3]

Roberts had no sooner hit the snow on Takur Gahr than the wheels were already in motion to go back for him. A young army captain by the name of Nate Self readied his QRF (Quick Reaction Force)—a platoon of elite Army Rangers—to "run to the guns" where Roberts battled for his life. You can read the full story in Nate's well-written and heart-wrenching book, *Two Wars*. Three Rangers and their Air Force Combat Controller brothers would give their lives that day to fulfill their vow to fellow soldiers. It was part of the warrior code, part of a fellowship made sacred by the spirit of self-sacrifice.

Because it's a demanding code, it's a rich fellowship. It's the sweet flavor of life-rending, soul-stretching camaraderie pounded out in the heat of life's adversities. Once tasted, it lingers with us for the rest of our lives and leaves us longing for more.

The power of friendship forged under adversity is one of life's greatest treasures. Once you've experienced it, you'll never be the same. And you hate to leave it.

One young soldier sat on his bunk in his tent in Iraq, head in his hands, reflecting sadly on what was about to happen to him. His tour of duty was done; he was heading home; his days in the army were coming to an end. You'd think he would be overjoyed. And on one hand he was anticipating it. After all, he would return to the world he knew best. A safe world filled with acquaintances, activities, a job, and even some fun.

But the tears running down his cheeks that day were not tears of joy. When one of his fellow soldiers asked him about the tears, he responded transparently: "I'm afraid I will never be this alive again, that I will never know this kind of purpose when I get up in the morning. Is my whole life going to be common from now on?"[4]

Purpose. Adversity. A transcendent cause. The fellowship of suffering. A fraternity of warriors. Whether one is facing lead bullets or spiritual missiles, the elements of battle are the same. And the sheer power of such friendship is life marking, life making, and lifesaving.

IRON ON IRON

God gives us three primary growth or change agents in our lives: His Word, His Spirit, and His people, our fellow Christian brothers. When I'm down, have lost perspective, or I'm in some kind of personal pain, I've noticed I don't read the Bible the same way. It's just words on a page. And the Bible tells me I'm capable of quenching the Spirit of God. But I've found that I can't get away from my friends in Christ. Not only will they not leave me, but they also won't let me go. Like medics on a battlefield, they are there to patch me up and keep me in the fight.

We've spoken about Prince Jonathan already. But I was recently struck by this young man's courageous, timely encouragement of his friend David. At the risk of his own life, he found David and his men while they were fugitives and on the run. Getting alone with his buddy David, Scripture says that Jonathan "helped him find strength in God." He told David, "Don't be afraid...You will be king over Israel, and I will be second to you" (1 Sam. 23:16–17, NIV). Jonathan took the trouble to find David, turned his discouraged friend's eyes back toward God, and gave him a positive vision of the future. What a friend!

Whether it's physical combat or spiritual warfare, the deepest friendships are *forged*. Look up that word. When metal is shaped for a specific usefulness, it's heated and hammered until it attains its effectiveness. Sounds to me a lot like the way the strongest friendships are made. The best of friendships often seem to come together under the greatest pressure.

My favorite proverb reflects some of the heat and friction of steel on steel, or iron on iron, to use the word from ancient Israel. "As iron sharpens iron, so one person sharpens another" (Prov. 27:17, NIV).

Think through the process of iron on iron, of blade on steel. What are the key elements of this process?

I'd like to suggest four, each beginning with the letter *A*. Forgive the alliteration, but never forget the powerful process. I don't recall where I first heard these four As, but I do know they've become something of a life message for me. They govern every meaningful friendship in my life.

Four As

Here are four elements that will help you develop that kind of close-knit, soul-to-soul, life-shaping friendship; four things to remember well:

- *Acceptance*
- *Affirmation*
- *Accountability*
- *Authority*

Four small words. Four huge realities.

Acceptance

A necessary power. Acceptance is the engine that drives and sustains the friendship. Paul directed the church to accept one another just as Christ accepted them (Rom. 15:7). Christ's acceptance was a gracious response that was open-handed, open-hearted, and unconditional—a "come as you are" invitation to a relationship. The relationship between Christ and His disciples was characterized by grace, truth, and forgiveness.

How does that apply to iron sharpening iron? Before steel can sharpen a blade, the two must be held together by a force greater than either. In the case of a knife the force is the hands of the guy sharpening the blade. The corresponding force in a masculine friendship is the power of acceptance. And acceptance is *powerful.*

You recall the old Boys Town USA poster of the two youngsters at the farmhouse steps, one on the shoulders of the other, seeking shelter from a threatening sky. The matron answering the door evidently remarks about the weighty load the older boy is carrying. The caption says it all: "He ain't heavy; he's my brother!" It's as though we're intended to understand that their relationship is so strong and mutually dependent that even gravity doesn't apply to it. By gum, he's going to carry his brother no matter what. And he won't allow anything to come between them, not even gravity. It's as though the older boy recognizes his brother wouldn't have made it to shelter if he hadn't carried him.

In a masculine friendship the power of acceptance is the enabling power. Acceptance will not allow any of the normal irritants (those that typically drive people apart) to apply to this friendship.

To illustrate, let me tell you about two of my own sons, now adults. In high school they were close enough in age to drive each other nuts. All the natural irritants between a sophomore and a senior applied—from misusing the brother's belongings to interfering with each other's schedules to you name it. There was more than enough testosterone to go around, and they could scrap with the best of them. Casual wrestling sometimes turned into serious contests. That's the way with brothers growing up. *But*—don't try to get between them. As the old proverb says, "A brother is born for adversity" (Prov. 17:17).

One day between classes at school, for some still unknown reason, the sophomore brother was "put upon" by a senior student, and a fight was in the making. A crowd gathered. Tension was high.

My son told me later, "Dad, I didn't know what to do. My brain was racing. 'Do I swing first? Beat a fast retreat? Try to talk my way out of this?'" Before he could put it together, something really fast came sprinting up the hallway where the fight was developing. That something charged through the crowd, inadvertently bumped some folks out of the way, and dragged the senior bully up against a locker. He immobilized the aggressor and informed him in no uncertain terms, "Don't fight with him; he's my brother, and you're going to have to deal with me first."

That pretty much says it all. That's the sheer power of acceptance. (I more recently learned, long years after the altercation, that after the older brother broke up the crowd he took the aggressor by the hair and unceremoniously led him to a nearby open courtyard for a "more detailed, pointed, and personal conversation." Ah, acceptance! It makes your life safer. And better. Thank God for big brothers.

Affirmation

A smoothing oil. We all understand that sharpening a blade often requires a honing oil. In terms of a masculine friendship that relational honing oil is affirmation. Affirmation has a potent calming effect on every relationship.

We all long for affirmation, and we're actually desperate for it. But you may have noticed that it's impossible to affirm yourself. You can talk to yourself about how good you are until you're blue in the face. But you still won't believe it. We thirst for affirmation outside ourselves. It must come from an authoritative source we recognize as such.

The military understands that. It's part of the purpose of the medals worn on Class A uniforms. That medal, granted by an authorized superior, says, "I was there. I saw what you did. You were outstanding. And I recognize and applaud you for it."

Affirmation makes you a better person. I will never forget my high school basketball coach. After one game when I was a sophomore, he slapped me on the butt and said, "You got seven rebounds, son! Way to go! I'll bet you next game you get ten." Well, ten rebounds was all I thought about for the whole week. Affirmation strengthened our relationship and motivated me to improve my half of it. (On the other hand, recall how much you disliked playing for a coach who only criticized.) Affirmation makes you a better man. I arrived at that high school a fairly timid kid, but by the time that coach finished with me, he'd made me into a warrior. Purely because of his affirmation I began to believe every loose ball was mine, and it showed up in the stats.

Accountability

A healthy friction. For iron to sharpen iron, there has to be a bit of friction. Friction creates heat. Now and then, given the right materials, sparks can even fly. In a masculine friendship the corresponding healthy friction is called accountability.

For your friendship to mature and contribute to your growth, it must eventually become one of mutual accountability. None of us has it all together. And any close relationship worth having long-term has to rise to the level of accountability.

Back in the nineties when *accountability* was the latest ministry buzzword, I thought it would be a good thing for all our staff pastors to get into accountability groups. We put all our names in a hat and teamed in groups of three. I'd just assumed I would end up with guys very similar to me, and we'd have a good time. I drew the church administrator and the pastor of counseling. Innocent enough.

But what do you know about administrators? They're detailed people, analytical people, precise people. And I am none of the above! Another word for detailed, analytical precision is *nitpicker*.

And what do you know about professional counselors? They're threateningly insightful. They like to ask lots of probing questions, and they love to impose sentence completion upon small groups, such as "Let's all complete this sentence: The last time I was really angry was when..." Another word for all that is *nosey*.

So I was trapped in a group with Misters Nosey and Nitpicky.

For the first several weeks it was horrible. We didn't know what to do or how to conduct an "accountability group." It was just a cool concept. Our group times were slow, boring, and accomplished nothing. The three of us were like dogs circling a fire hydrant, with no one actually doing anything.

At about five weeks things changed. One of the three of us courageously decided to take a risk. The trauma of transparency is real, but without it there is no real authenticity. A recent personal temptation was shared. The authenticity transformed our times together. The doorway to meaningful, transparent, and spiritual interaction had been opened wide. What had once been the worst hour of the week became our most anticipated hour.

Here's what we discovered: all our shortcomings and liabilities were "common to man," to use the Bible's words. And that all our assets or strengths were "gifts from God," to use the same perspective. We finally realized that since everything good or positive about us was a gift from God, and that since everything bad or negative about us was shared by every man, then hey, we had no reason to hide from one another! Transparency increased and so did maturity. We were able to become open-hearted, mutually encouraging, seriously transparent fellow warriors in the battle called life. Our lives, our marriages, our parenting, our families, and our friendship experienced fresh growth.

The accountability group had turned on a dime. And that dime was honesty.

Authority

A skillful angle. For a blade to be sharpened by steel, it must make contact at just the right angle. If the angle is too steep, or not steep enough, it becomes an exercise in frustration. (Which is why I ask my brother-in-law to sharpen any knife; I just don't have the knack.) The relational element that corresponds to that angle is authority—knowing just when it's right to pull the trigger on the matter at hand. Too much or too little accomplishes nothing.

I vividly recall a pack trip into the Eagle Cap Wilderness years ago. My best friend, of over forty years now, had horses and mules, and our families loved to spend a week in July tucked away in the mountains, ten miles from the end of the nearest road. You can imagine the trip was a bit arduous with plenty of potential for "train wrecks" along the way. As a young man at the time, I mistakenly thought the point of a vacation was to "Get there!" by hook or crook or shoving or pushing, and maybe even a little shouting; just get there fast, with no foolin' around. (I was all too frequently an idiot in my younger years—and I'll bet you were too; it's pretty much common to man).

Well, we finally arrived at the campsite—dusty, tired, and more than a little worn out. After setting up camp, preparing dinner, and tucking the kids into the tents for the night, the wives sat in the "kitchen," and John and I hiked up the hillside a bit to watch some elk feed down a draw on the opposite side. We were sitting on a chunk of granite, when my friend, certainly unexpectedly from my perspective, turned toward me and with some fire in his eyes said, "I don't ever want to hear you talk to one of your sons that way again!"

Now, if it had been anyone else, I would likely have blown it off or pushed back some. Not with John. He's my true friend. We'd been together for years. He had accepted me, affirmed me, held me accountable, and he'd earned the right to be an authority in my life. Our friendship was always full of grace and truth. I "saluted and executed," as we say. He was right, I was wrong, and I needed to change. And I also needed to make it right with my son.

FIND THOSE FRIENDS

Four As. There you have it—a full-on masculine friendship grounded on the bedrock of biblical relationships, where there's acceptance and affirmation, all the while exercising accountability and authority. It's biblical. And it works.

Never go into battle alone. Find a friend, or several, who can embrace and live out those four As with you.

How do you find them? Here's my recommended approach:

- Take the initiative; be a man. Manhood personifies initiative.

- Pray. God doesn't give us stones when we ask for bread. And He loves to answer such a prayer. After all, this kind of friendship was all His idea in the first place. His is the original friendship—Father, Son, Holy Spirit.

- Develop a target list of candidates, men you've noticed. You may not even know their names. Pray some more about the targets.

- Take the initiative. Buy two copies of the same book. Approach your candidate, give him one copy, and offer to buy lunch in a couple days. Suggest you each read a chapter and maybe chat about it at lunch. If nothing more ever comes of it, tell him there's nothing to lose. At least he got a free book and a free lunch out of it.

- If nothing comes of it, start the process over—until it "takes" with someone.

I had one guy tell me he tried my suggested approach and the first nine guys all turned him down. He was one discouraged puppy. But he later informed me the tenth guy "took"—and his life hasn't been the same.

Every Ranger needs a Ranger buddy. Every fighter pilot needs a wingman. And every man needs a man friend.

Joshua and Caleb were glad they did it. David and Jonathan were an unstoppable team. *Together is better.* Every intelligent man knows that.

And think of it: on top of the good in this life, Joshua and Caleb have all eternity together to sit around heaven's campfires and swap the best of life stories.

Find a friend, my friend. You need it. And he needs it, even if he doesn't know it yet. Be strong. Be persistent. Go for it. Live it. And relive it.

RELIVING

Because it's so potent, old soldiers who saw combat together love to gather together. They call them reunions. There is union. And there is reliving. And, yes—to a depth unknown to others—a re-loving. Sometimes they even use the word *love* in conversations with one another. More often they simply sit in one another's presence and when one of those quiet, reflective moments occurs, they sit silent but reliving, and re-knowing, and re-loving. And if you look closely, you'll see every eye a little more glazed over than age alone can account for.

One Vietnam veteran said it well for every gathering of old warriors. Michael Norman's sentiments are stated so simply yet majestically, I suggest you remove any headgear and bow your head as you read these virtually sacred words:

> I now know why men who have been to war yearn to reunite. Not to tell stories or look at old pictures. Not to laugh or weep on one another's knee. Comrades gather because they long to be with men who once acted their best, men who suffered and sacrificed, who were stripped raw, right down to their humanity.
>
> I did not pick these men. They were delivered by fate and the US Marine Corps. But I know them in a way I know no other men. I have never since given anyone such trust. They were willing to guard something more precious than my life. They would have carried my reputation, the memory of me. It was part of the bargain we all made, the reason we were so willing to die for one another.
>
> As long as I have memory, I will think of them all, every day. I am sure that when I leave this world, my last thoughts will be of my family—and my comrades, such good men.[5]

I can well imagine Caleb and Joshua reflecting similarly.

Who can forget the *Band of Brothers* closing interview with Dick Winters, the real-life company commander of Easy Company, of the 506th Parachute Infantry Regiment? Theirs is the story so well portrayed in that miniseries. In the interview Winters was reading—with a tear in his eye and a tremor in his voice—a letter he'd received from Easy Company's Sergeant Mike Ranney. Ranney wrote, "My grandson asked me the other day...'Grandpa, were you a hero in the war?' Grandpa said, 'No, but I served in a company of heroes.'"[6]

You and I would do well to take the lesson to heart—every

man needs a soul brother with whom to ride the river. Every man belongs in a *company*. Companions.

Most of us will never see the mountains of Afghanistan or the sands of Iraq. We'll not likely face the bullets of a hate-filled terrorist. But every single one of us, in one form or another, faces multiple battles on a daily basis. And the results are just as far-reaching, maybe further, than physical combat. Battles have a way of impacting generations.

Since all of life is a battle, and this world is a war zone, every man gets hit in one way or another along the way. Most of those battles are spiritual at their core. We can call it mental stress, or emotional pressure, or whatever term we may choose. But bottom line, it's all a spiritual matter. Whether it's a financial pressure, a sexual temptation, a power struggle, a tough marriage, a difficult child, an impossible job—whatever it is, it's ultimately spiritual at the core. And every one of us needs a "band of brothers" to face off against the enemy of our souls. Every one of us needs a fellow warrior beside us big enough to carry us when we get hit. We all long for a fellow soldier who'll stick with us through thick and thin, who'll never walk away, never leave us behind.

It was true with Joshua and Caleb. And it was true in spades for two other great Old Testament warriors, David and Jonathan. (Again, I encourage you to read their story, beginning in 1 Samuel 14.)

And it is true for me. I am fortunate to have several such fellow warriors in my life. Men who know me, my strengths and weaknesses. Men who love me anyway. Men who will not let me fall. Men who will carry me when I get hit. Men who would come if I called at 3:00 in the morning. Let me introduce you to one of them.

I've known Lt. Gen. William G. (Jerry) Boykin for years now. I'd do anything for him. And he for me. Though we live on opposite coasts, three time zones apart, we are determined to live and relive our friendship. Several times a year we arrange our schedules so as to be together. And every single such time always involves heartfelt, soulish conversation. Every encounter we have is a mutually strengthening spiritual experience. He says I teach him theology. I say he teaches me the power of prayer. Let him teach you a bit about the sheer power of prayer as well as the ethics of soldiers fighting wars. That's what these next chapters are all about.

Chapter 10

THE POWER OF THE TEN-SECOND PRAYER

Finding God's Help Amid the Battle
by General Boykin

The effective prayer of a righteous
man can accomplish much.
• JAMES 5:16 •

UNFORGETTABLE MOMENTS. MOMENTS of danger and desperation. And in the midst of them, I have experienced my prayers
being answered by an omnipotent and sovereign God.

Let me tell you about some of them.

THROUGH THE FIRE

Dasht-e Kavir, Iran—April 24, 1980—22:30 hours

I stood watching in disbelief as flames reached skyward into
the darkness of the Iranian desert. The Delta Force was here—in
this remote spot about a hundred miles from the Iranian capital,
Tehran—because we'd been directed by US president Jimmy Carter
to rescue fifty-two American diplomats being held by a group of
radical students at the US Embassy in the capital. This was a refueling stop before we made our final night assault on the embassy to

bring our fellow Americans back to their families and to an American public that was eager to welcome them home.

Now our hopes had turned to disappointment and desperation as we gazed at the burning wreckage of a US Air Force C-130 and a US Navy RH-53 helicopter, which had collided on the ground after refueling. As the helo pilot had attempted to reposition after completing his refueling from fuel bladders in the C-130, he'd lost his equilibrium—he "went vertigo," in aviation lingo. Lifting off, he'd lost control and crashed onto the C-130, slamming into the top and left side of the cargo plane. The eruption was immediate; aviation fuel exploded in the helo and engulfed the C-130 in a massive ball of high-octane fire.

Initially I turned to run as I felt the heat and saw pieces of metal flying out into the desert. But I didn't go far, only a few steps, before I became fully aware of the presence of the Holy Spirit. I even sensed Him calling me to stop and turn back toward the wreckage. I spun around, knowing that an explosion would come quickly when the fuel in the C-130 finally ignited. Then the reality hit me: forty-five Delta Force men were trapped inside the wreckage with no way out and no chance to survive the fire. And I could not help them.

Only eighteen hours earlier I had stood with these men in an old Russian MiG base in Wadi Qena, Egypt, as we prayed for God to go with us on this mission. I'd led the prayer that morning before we launched the operation, petitioning God to keep His hand of protection upon us. And now I was watching those same men die a fiery death while I stood helplessly by.

It took only seconds before I instinctively began pleading with God for the lives of these men. My prayer was that of a desperate man who knew that only God could save those forty-five souls in that wreckage. "Oh God," I pleaded, "please spare them! They trusted You, Lord! In Jesus's name, bring them out alive. *God, I'm asking You not to let these men die.*"

It was all I could do—and the most important thing I could do.

My plea was sincere. They needed a miracle, and there was no time for a great oration or for promises of what I would do in return if God would come through for them. There wasn't even time for me to go through my normal routine of thanking God for everything He'd already done for me in the past, or for telling Him what a worthless sinner I was (as if He didn't know). And no time for pomp or style or fancy words. Those men needed this miracle *now*.

So there it was, my ten-second prayer. And it was all I had to offer. "Over to You now, God."

Suddenly the right troop door of that C-130 opened. I could barely see through the flames, but instantly I saw the miracle take shape. Forty-five men jumped one by one through those flames and out onto the desert floor, then ran from the crash like a redbone hound on the scent of a raccoon.

"*Yes, Lord—thank You, Lord!* You are so awesome, God!" I spoke the words aloud as I ran to greet these men and to help direct them to the safety of the other C-130s some distance away.

MALFUNCTIONING CHUTE

Fort Bragg, North Carolina—July 10, 1982

I was falling at one hundred twenty miles per hour toward the drop zone, anticipating the opening shock I would soon feel as my canopy opened only a second or so after I pulled the rip cord. It was my third free-fall jump, and I'd had no real training. I was doing something really dumb, jumping without proper training. I was OK as long as everything went well, but I wasn't at all sure how to handle any of the myriad malfunctions that could occur on a free-fall jump. Although I'd been trained for static-line jumping, this was different and considerably more dangerous.

As I approached the four-thousand-foot point, I prepared to grasp the rip cord with my right hand while bringing my left hand in close to my helmet, in order to remain symmetric and stable. I pulled and resumed my spread-eagle position as the parachute unfurled from the pack on my back.

I felt the opening shock as I expected, but something was wrong. I couldn't raise my head to look up and check my canopy. One of the risers—the straps connecting jumper to parachute—was preventing me from looking up because it was pressing down pretty hard on my neck. Furthermore, I was spinning and falling much faster than I should have been.

Finally I craned my neck to a position to be able to see what was going on. I had two canopies, as both my main and reserve canopies had deployed simultaneously due to a malfunction in the automatic opening device (AOD). I knew this was one of the most dangerous malfunctions in free-fall parachuting, because the canopies frequently entangle with each other, leaving the jumper with no lift and normally resulting in a fatality. Although my canopies weren't entangled, there was great potential for them to do so. Regardless, I was spinning and falling fast since the two canopies were stealing air from each other, causing me to turn in a clockwise direction with very little lift to provide for a safe landing.

This was going to hurt when I hit the ground. Would I survive? It was no sure thing that I'd live through this one. And if I did, it was a pretty safe bet that I was going to break something—most likely my back.

So I began a desperate prayer of only a few words: "Lord, I need Your help. I ask that You bring me down safely. Let me survive this, Lord. In Jesus's name I ask."

Finished with the prayer, I now knew I was going to hit the ground in about three seconds. Suddenly I saw green below me. *Trees*—right under me. This was going to be worse than I thought.

I sailed right through several forty-foot pines, then hit the ground.

It was a surprisingly soft landing. My feet hit, then I fell to my knees, banging my right knee on a stump. I was unhurt. What happened? How could this be? I should have crashed.

I looked up and was amazed at the sight of my canopy hanging from the top of one of the pines. As I passed through the trees, it had snagged and broken my fall. I was literally saved by a pine tree.

Well, yeah, I know how the tree got there. And how my canopy found it. It was the hand of the Almighty, once again saving a knucklehead who had more courage than brains.

My prayer was short but it was sincere, and God heard it and responded. I had a bruised knee to remind me of how dumb I was and how good He is—but I walked off the drop zone that morning, thanking Him for His help.

SURROUNDED

Bakaara Market, Mogadishu, Somalia—October 3, 1993

The battle of the Bakaara Market was raging, as ninety-nine American soldiers were surrounded by thousands of drug-crazed Somali militia. It was, at the time, the toughest battle the American military had been in since Vietnam, and I was commanding the ground troops from my tactical operations center (TOC) at our base on the airfield in Somalia's capital city, Mogadishu. I was blocks away in the relative safety of the TOC, while my men were in a desperate situation as they fought for their lives against heavily armed fighters who had them completely surrounded.

The Task Force Ranger helos were making run after run up and down the streets, firing rockets and miniguns, trying to kill as many enemy as they could. But there were so many of them, and they just kept coming.

The plan to get our men out was dependent on other UN forces such as the Malaysians and the Pakistanis, who had tanks and armored personnel carriers (APCs). Because of the language barriers they were slow in mobilizing and even slower in understanding what we needed them to do. Could my men hold out until we could get to them? I wasn't sure. They were continuing to take casualties and were already treating a few critically injured comrades.

We needed a miracle here, and I knew where to find it. I needed to stay on the radio with the various commanders, including the aircrews, but I also needed to speak to God.

I was torn. I looked to my left, and there in the TOC was my chaplain. I stood up and motioned for my operations officer to take over for a minute while I stepped out of the TOC. I grabbed the chaplain by the arm, saying nothing as I led him out into the darkness. He wasn't sure what was happening.

The line of sandbags directly in front of the TOC door was a perfect altar. Without needing an explanation from me, the chaplain knelt beside me, and we pleaded with God for a miracle. Our prayer was no more than ten seconds, but we prayed with the deep passion of desperate men.

We finished our prayer and returned immediately inside the TOC. I resumed my duties and spent the longest night of my life running the operation to get those men out of Mogadishu. The Lord showed us favor. He answered our prayer and brought the men to safety the next morning, just as the sun was rising over the city. Although we suffered both dead and wounded as a result of the fight that night, the bulk of the guys were still combat ready. God heard and answered the short prayer of two desperate men.

BECAUSE HE'S GOD

Desperate prayers, answered so amazingly by an amazing God. Did God answer those prayers because I'm a good Christian man? I strongly doubt that.

Did He answer them because I'm a righteous man? Nope, don't think so.

So then, what's up?

It's simple. *He is God.* He doesn't answer prayers because we deserve to have them answered; otherwise, none of us would get a prayer answered.

I'm not sure about others, but from a spiritual perspective I'm not a good man. I'm flawed and sinful by nature. But I've committed my life to Jesus Christ, and in return He has promised to wipe my slate clean despite my sinful nature. Furthermore He has promised that He will never leave me nor forsake me, no matter how rebellious or how degenerate my behavior is.

That's what they call *grace*. Grace is unmerited favor, and it's not a human concept. It is divine, and only God really understands it, because He created it to help each of us get beyond our sinful nature.

Some have asked me if I pray about every decision that I make. The simple answer is no. I don't consider myself a righteous man nor a particularly good Christian, but I'm committed to doing my best to walk with Jesus Christ daily. There are days when He must be pretty disappointed in my behavior, but He still keeps me close to Him.

I pray every day; sometimes for longer periods than others. As a result of talking with God each day, I don't feel that I must consult Him immediately and absolutely before every decision or action. I'm trusting Him to guide me and to speak into my life as I try to live a life that reflects Him through me.

But many times I find significant opportunities for those ten-second prayers, sustaining my life and faith and pushing me forward along the pathway He's set out for me.

Assured Answers

Remember the story of the two thieves on the crosses next to Jesus? It's important that we remember all three crosses on that hill called Golgotha ("The Skull") on the day Jesus died.

Jesus was in the center, with two other men being crucified on either side of Him, sharing in the indescribable agony of this horrible method of execution. We can assume these two other fellows were pretty bad guys, since they were condemned to death for their crimes. No doubt they were scoundrels, altogether guilty.

One of the thieves mocked Jesus and challenged Him—if He really was the Son of God, He should get off the cross and save all three of them.

But the other thief rebuked his partner in crime. "Do you not even fear God?" this second thief asked, "since you are under the same sentence of condemnation? And we indeed are suffering justly, for we are receiving what we deserve for our deeds; but *this man has done nothing wrong*" (Luke 23:39–41). He recognized the truth about Jesus.

This second thief then turned to the man on the center cross. "Jesus, remember me when You come in Your kingdom!" The man in the center answered him with something we all need to be reminded of. Jesus responded, "Truly I say to you, today *you shall be with Me in Paradise*" (Luke 23:42–43).

Wow! Think about what Jesus did *not* tell this man. Jesus didn't ask if he'd been baptized, paid his tithes, or done good works. That didn't matter to Christ. What *did* matter was that this thief was simply recognizing Jesus as the Savior and accepting Him as such. From his heart the thief was asking Jesus for forgiveness and for the assurance of eternity with God. And Jesus gave him the desire of his heart.

That's *grace*—and we can all experience it.

Oh, it's important that we're baptized and that we pay our tithes, and that we put our faith into action and do good things for God's children. But *knowing* Christ as our Savior—and being in a relationship with Him that assures us He hears and answers our prayers—is never about how good or pious we are. It's all about *who He is*. He's a loving and forgiving God who takes us just as we are, regardless of all the flaws and warts and stains on our lives.

So does God hear every prayer we pray as believers in Him? *He sure does.*

Does He answer every prayer we pray? *Yep again.* Sometimes He says yes, sometimes He says no, and many times He says, "Wait."

All things are done—and all prayers are answered—according to God's loving grace and His will in our lives. We may not understand

His plan or His reasons for how our prayers are answered, but rest assured that God has a plan.

And that plan definitely includes an ongoing relationship between you and Him that is marked every day by your prayers...and His answers.

☆ Chapter 11 ☆

THE WARRIOR'S ETHICS

More Than Words
by General Boykin

The soldier's trade, if it is to mean anything at
all, has to be anchored to an unshakeable code
of honor. Otherwise, those of us who follow
the drums become nothing more than a bunch
of hired assassins walking around in gaudy
clothes...disgrace to God and mankind.[1]
• PRUSSIAN MAJ. GEN. CARL VON CLAUSEWITZ •

HE BATTLE RAGED for eighteen hours in the sweltering equato-
rial heat of a city in total chaos, where anarchy was the natural
state of the society.

Let me take you back again to Mogadishu, Somalia, on that
October day in 1993. The city was filled with the sounds of AK-47s
and rocket-propelled grenades being fired by thousands of drug-
crazed Somali militiamen, all of whom wanted to kill an American
soldier from the elite unit known as Task Force Ranger.

But the Rangers were giving more than they were taking, and the
volume of their fire was even more impressive as they hammered
away with their M-4 carbines, M-240G machine guns, and M-203
grenade launchers. American helicopters zipped low above the
roofs of the buildings, delivering a steady staccato of 7.62-millimeter

minigun rounds. The "whomp" of the 2.75-inch rockets being fired from the small helos known as Little Bird Guns kept the militia running for cover.

And when that eighteen-hour gunfight ended the next morning, fifteen of America's finest warriors were dead, and another seventy-plus were wounded. The battle cost the Somali militias an estimated eleven hundred dead or wounded.

INESCAPABLE VALUES

Chronicled in the book and movie *Black Hawk Down,* this battle was about more than just killing or capturing the enemy. For Task Force Ranger it was about personal commitment, honor, courage, selflessness, and living up to the values and ethics of the Ranger Creed—part of which says, "I will never leave a fallen comrade to fall into the hands of the enemy."[2]

The truth of the matter that day was that America's finest warriors had completed their primary mission hours earlier. They'd been sent to capture several senior members of the Habr Gidr clan militia. Within the first hour that task had been accomplished and the captives had been evacuated back to the Task Force base at the Mogadishu airfield. The fight continued because a Black Hawk had been shot down during the operation, killing the pilot and copilot and injuring four more men who were riding in the helo when it crashed. The four passengers had survived the crash with various injuries and had all been evacuated in helos flown by courageous crews who landed, amidst a hail of small-arms fire, to save their buddies. Only the dead aviators remained to be evacuated.

But there was a problem. The dead pilot and copilot were trapped inside the twisted wreckage of the UH-60 Black Hawk and couldn't be removed without the use of cutting saws and other mechanical devices, which weren't available at the scene of the crash. The Task Force had two options: leave the bodies and get everyone to the safety of their base at the airfield, or stay and fight until appropriate tools for extracting the two bodies could be brought to the crash.

Casualties were mounting inside the small perimeter that had been established to defend the crash site. Militia from around the city converged, not wanting to miss this fight and the chance to be part of a great militia victory over the hated Rangers.

Task Force Ranger was rapidly being surrounded by thousands of armed Somalis with only one mission: *kill the Americans.*

The longer the Americans stayed, the tougher the fight became, increasing in intensity by the minute and resulting in more dead and wounded on both sides.

The Task Force knew they could grab their wounded and start fighting their way out to safety using their reliable helicopter gunships to clear a path for them as they worked their way out of the city. It was the best way to prevent further loss of life among their small fighting force. There was nothing they could do now for the dead men in the crash, and their mounting casualties were reducing their combat effectiveness. Ammo was getting low; so were water and medical supplies.

They really needed to go only a few blocks to be back inside territory controlled by United Nations Forces from multiple countries. But every man there that day knew that they wouldn't be leaving until they'd recovered the bodies of their comrades—even knowing that this required a relief force to fight its way into the crash site, bringing the mechanical devices needed to rip apart the downed aircraft and recover the bodies. No one was under any illusion about what they were going to face if they stayed and fought.

With more militia pouring in, and their own supplies dwindling, the Rangers made the only choice they could. They stayed.

The Ranger Creed was more than words to them; it was their identity, culture, heritage, ethos, and their ethical standard. Some would call it the embodiment of their values in a statement that every man could recite from memory. For these men it was a reflection of their warrior spirit.

A Reminder: Who We Are

The Ranger Handbook has been a handy guide for soldiers for decades. Every soldier has one and considers it a necessity when planning and executing small unit operations.

Replete with the "how-to" for nearly everything the small unit soldier will encounter, the handbook also articulates the Ranger Creed—a creed that is inculcated into every Ranger unit at every level. Rangers live by it. It becomes an ethos for each of them.

Rangers recite the creed regularly, including during combat operations. As the Third Ranger Battalion was on their final approach to the Rio Hato airfield in Panama on the night of December 20, 1989, these paratroopers knew they were about to jump into a hornet's nest that would likely result in some of them not coming home alive.

As the aircraft approached the drop zone, the battalion command sergeant major shuffled to the rear of the aircraft and began to recite the first stanza of the Ranger Creed. Soon every Ranger was following his lead. The words spewed out in unison and could be heard over the noise of the roaring C-130 engines as the entire planeload of Rangers recited their heartfelt statement of who they are. They were encouraging, strengthening, and reassuring one another.

When the last man exited the aircraft that night, the Rangers were ready for a fight, and their subsequent actions brought them a resounding victory against the defense forces of the Panamanian military dictator Manuel Noriega.

These young warriors were well trained and equipped, and fully prepared to take on the enemy at Rio Hato that night. They had rehearsed their plan repeatedly and had full confidence in their leadership at all levels. So what was the point of reciting the Ranger Creed in those final moments before they jumped into the darkness of the Panamanian sky over an airfield surrounded by a tropical jungle? Was it a type of false bravado? Or just a distraction to divert their attention away from personal fear and apprehension?

No, it was a reminder of *who they are*, through a statement of the ethics by which they live. Ultimately that creed lays down the ethical code that each man has embraced as a way of life.

THE RANGER CREED

Let's take a look at the entire creed and assess what it really means.

Recognizing that I volunteered as a Ranger, fully knowing the hazards of my chosen profession, I will always endeavor to uphold the prestige, honor, and high esprit de corps of the Rangers.

Acknowledging the fact that a Ranger is a more elite Soldier who arrives at the cutting edge of battle by land, sea, or air, I accept the fact that as a Ranger my country expects me to move further, faster and fight harder than any other Soldier.

Never shall I fail my comrades I will always keep myself mentally alert, physically strong and morally straight and I will shoulder more than my share of the task whatever it may be, one-hundred-percent and then some.

Gallantly will I show the world that I am a specially selected and well-trained Soldier. My courtesy to superior officers, neatness of dress and care of equipment shall set the example for others to follow.

Energetically will I meet the enemies of my country. I shall defeat them on the field of battle for I am better trained and will fight with all my might. Surrender is not a Ranger word. I will never leave a fallen comrade to fall into the hands of the enemy and under no circumstances will I ever embarrass my country.

Readily will I display the intestinal fortitude required to fight on to the Ranger objective and complete the mission though I be the lone survivor.[3]

Warriors are not simply people trained to fight. A warrior fights for a transcendent cause. A warrior is imbued with a set of ethical standards that are reflected in his actions.

In World War II the brutality of the Japanese during their occupation of China and Korea and much of Southeast Asia, along with the annihilation of the Jews by Hitler's troops in Europe, together reflect the actions of people who are trained to fight yet have none of the requisite ethics that make them warriors. The warrior has at his core an understanding of right and wrong. He doesn't see warfare as a personal issue between himself and the enemy across the battlefield from him. The warrior's values include respect for his enemy despite the fact that they're engaged in a lethal struggle where ultimately one of them is going to die or surrender.

Always conscious of the consequences and impact of his actions in battle, the warrior stays within the boundaries of his ethical code, even in the toughest of battles. He must live with the consequences of his actions. Killing or subduing the enemy is his mission, and he must be adept at doing so without a notion of revenge or personal vendetta. His transcendent cause, the reason he fights, must prevail.

Again, being trained to fight is not what makes a man a warrior. Confident in his purpose, the true warrior prepares for and enters battle with a strong sense of the righteousness of what he's doing. He fights because he believes in his cause, and he fights in a manner that ensures that his honor and that of his team are preserved.

The warrior stands and fights when others flee in fear because of his commitment to the cause. The warrior runs to the guns and the sound of battle because he knows his purpose. The warrior is not a mercenary. He doesn't serve for money. Nor does he fight solely because he enjoys the thrill of combat, or because of the adrenaline rush prompted by the sounds of battle and the smell of cordite.

Unlike the mercenary, who may decide the risk is too great to continue the fight, the warrior is guided by his ethical obligation to fulfill his commitment of service. Risk is something he accepts as the norm, and it's never a deterrent, only a factor.

Deadly Hesitation

On an April day in 1999 two students named Dylan Klebold and Eric Harris walked into Columbine High School in Colorado and began shooting their classmates, ultimately killing thirteen people and wounding twenty-one others.

Videos of the incident show law enforcement officers on the scene huddled along the side of the school as the two killers inside systematically moved from room to room, selecting their victims. Waiting for more information on what was happening inside, the sworn officers delayed their entry, giving Klebold and Harris more time to kill. The warrior ethos wasn't evident that day among those who were sworn to defend the public. Rather than waiting for more information, the officers should have run to the guns. The battle was inside where people were dying. It's the duty of the warrior to take risks if he believes in the cause for which he serves.

In this case the risks of being injured or killed themselves should have been overridden by the sworn obligation of the police and deputies to defend the innocent. Any delay in accomplishing that objective should be unacceptable, even if it was the result of orders from the leader in charge of the operation. Everyone involved should be focused on saving the lives of the helpless regardless of the risks. Some may argue that disobeying orders could have resulted in punishment for the officers. The question really should be whether their first obligation should have been saving lives or obeying orders that impede their ability to accomplish that mission. I leave that for the reader to ponder, but for me the answer is easy: *run to the guns.*

THE RIGHT THING, REGARDLESS

It is common and understandable for us to think of warriors as people in uniform, either military or law enforcement. Yet every person can be a warrior if he possesses the commitment and values of the warrior. If he's guided by a set of ethical guidelines that prompts him to take action and demonstrate courage, he qualifies as a warrior. Anyone who approaches life with a determination to face difficult situations as a warrior, knowing right from wrong, doing the right thing, and being willing to act according to a warrior code of ethics is a warrior.

Conversely, those who serve only their own self-interest and who see nothing in life worth sacrificing for are the antithesis of the warrior.

Sadly, America has far too many people who just can't grasp the warrior code of ethics. It's incredible how many crimes against innocent people are observed by bystanders, in proximity to the incident, who do nothing to stop it. When a person walks by a mugging or a rape and does nothing to stop it, he can hardly consider himself a warrior. But the man who does his best to stop a crime against his neighbor, even at the risk of being attacked himself, is himself a true warrior. His code of ethics demands that he do the right thing regardless of the risks. He knows what must be done and doesn't hesitate. He could never live with himself nor find peace of mind if he failed to do what his ethical code demanded.

There are numerous cases in America in recent years of military veterans and just plain patriotic citizens who have been told to remove an American flag they were displaying at their home.[4] In many cases they've refused to do so because of their fundamental belief in their right as an American to fly the national colors. The warrior spirit rises up in them, and they stand for principle in spite of the consequences.

Judge Roy Moore refused to remove the Ten Commandments from the Supreme Court chambers in Alabama. Judge Moore, the court's chief justice, stood on his principles and fundamental beliefs, showing the warrior side of his character. He was removed from the court in November 2003 as a result of his actions.[5] But his ethical code and his values were more important to him than keeping his position.

The pastor who stands in his pulpit and speaks biblical truth when others are compromising on the fundamentals of the gospel of Christ is also a warrior. He answers to a higher commander than man, and he serves for a transcendent cause. His ethics derive from faith, and his motives derive from knowledge of God's expectations of him.

Parents who care enough about their children to discipline them and to hold them to high standards—even when the children object or rebel—are also demonstrating a warrior ethos.

An ethical code is something each person must develop. Each of us should spend time assessing our values and establishing such a code for ourselves.

It begins by determining what our transcendent cause is. We need to decide what price we're willing to pay for what we value. What risks are we willing to take for our beliefs and for those things we hold dear?

If our lives are all about serving our own interests, we'll come up short on the warrior scale. But if we truly see ourselves as part of something worth sacrificing for and taking risks for, and our actions reflect our commitment to serving the greater cause, then we're warriors.

THE EVIDENCE, IN BLOOD

In Mogadishu, hours after the battle ended there on October 4, 1993, I stood in the Task Force Ranger compound awaiting the arrival of a five-ton truck that was bringing our casualties back from the fight. It had been a long night, and I'd prayed many times through the battle for protection for my troops. As the Delta Force commander,

I was responsible for all these warriors, since they were all under my command—whether they were Rangers, SEALS, Aviators, or Delta Force.

My immediate commander, Major General Bill Garrison, was inside the command post that day answering a barrage of questions from Washington. I saw the truck approach the gate of our small fenced area, and I began to move forward to meet it. What I saw wasn't something I was ready for. In the truck bed were the bodies of the dead. Lying on top of them were the wounded.

Slowly and deliberately I moved closer to help. When the truck's tailgate was lowered, the blood of my soldiers poured out like water, splashing on the concrete of the airfield apron.

I choked back tears. My heart was breaking at the sight of bloody, mangled bodies filling the truck bed.

I stood and watched as the dead and wounded were carefully unloaded. I smelled the stench—blood, urine, feces...and death.

Quietly in my mind and heart I pondered many issues. "What kind of men are these? What did they die for? And Where does America find men like this?"

This was war in its ugliest form, and the carnage I gazed at there wasn't easy to understand. These were great young men who had so much life to live, yet fifteen of them were gone forever. Others were critically wounded.

I struggled to grasp it all.

Later I was reminded of John 15:13: "Greater love hath no man than this, that a man lay down his life for his friends" (KJV).

That said it all. Before me was the evidence that there still exists a warrior class who believe some things are worth fighting and dying for. They gave their lives willingly.

The Ranger regimental motto is the Latin phrase *Sua Sponte*—"On my own accord."[6] Well, here was the evidence that some men still lived by an ethical code—willingly, freely, on their own accord. *They were warriors.*

My further thoughts: "O God, why would You honor me with

the responsibility for men like this? I'm not worthy to command these men or even to consider myself one of them. But Lord, I'm so proud to be among them, for I know the true meaning of the word *warrior.*"

Those warriors in Mogadishu were no different than any of us who truly want to be warriors. They defined themselves by an ethical code and made a commitment to live by it. They knew what price they were willing to pay for that commitment.

Remember that these men are our sons, brothers, cousins, and neighbors. They came from the same small towns and big cities that we did. The difference is that they found their "cause" and were given the opportunity to go the distance.

I can assure you that none of the troops who lived through the battle in Mogadishu have any regrets about staying in the fight that day. They sleep well at night—as the warrior heart continues to beat in each of them, even as they continue to remember and mourn the loss of the brothers they loved.

Chapter 12

JUST WAR

Is This Really Worth It?

by General Boykin

And what does the LORD require of you
but to do justice, to love kindness, and
to walk humbly with your God?
• MICAH 6:8 •

T HE GREAT FAITH hall of fame, Hebrews chapter 11, indicates that spiritual faith accomplishes incredible physical feats: from walls collapsing to waters parting, from conquering kingdoms to quenching fires and dodging swords—yes, even to the specific point of violent physical combat and becoming "mighty in war and putting foreign armies to flight" (Heb. 11:34).

It seems reasonable, therefore, to conclude that spiritual warfare and physical combat are essentially two sides of the same coin. The physical is an expression of the spiritual. The material world, including combat, is an expression of the realities of the spiritual world. It seems that the heroes of our faith, this "great cloud of witnesses" surrounding us, saw little difference between the two worlds and warfare. The unchanging principles of "justice and righteousness" rule over conflict in both the physical and spiritual realms.

Perhaps it is this singular reality—the blending of the two

worlds—that is part of the reason God chose to describe one of the Bible's greatest spiritual heroes and most physical warriors—King David—as having "a heart of integrity." (See Psalm 78:72.) David's heart is described as a singular whole. It was an integer, an undivided unit. For David the world of swords, caves, blood, and battles was one with his world of worship, fellowship with God, and spiritual health. Is this not why David exulted, "By thee I have run through a troop; and by my God have I leaped over a wall" (Ps. 18:29, KJV)?

Perhaps a similar parallel is seen in 1 Chronicles 11 and 12, which list the unit rosters of Israel's greatest warriors in David's army. As noted earlier, certain phrases are repeated throughout these warrior chapters, phrases that seem to bear an intimate relationship, such as "mighty men of valor" and "according to the word of the Lord." Valor and God's truth are related. It seems a major point of the chapters is to indicate that "right makes might."

The closing chapters of the last book of the Bible, the Revelation of Jesus Christ, suggest similar parallels in the worlds of spiritual warfare and physical combat. Revelation 19:11 reads: "And I saw heaven opened, and behold, a white horse, and He who sat upon it is called Faithful and True, and *in righteousness He judges and wages war*." The immediate context is clearly one of extremely violent physical combat. But the larger context, the conclusion of all of Scripture, is clearly the conclusion of the entire spiritual history of Scripture. In the end the King of heaven and Lord of lords brings earth's history to a spiritual and physical conclusion in the same context of battle, both spiritual and physical.

Spiritual warfare in your life and mine is governed by the same principles that directed the lives of the heroes of the faith who have gone before us. Warfare, whether spiritual or physical, is to be waged in righteousness and justice.

Warfare is as old as the human race and will be a constant condition as long as men govern themselves. Given such a prevalence of war, one will find all sorts of views on warfare among the nations and societies on Earth. Those views range from total pacifism to extreme and open aggressiveness.

Into this mix, philosophers for millennia have debated the concept known as *just war*—war that is considered morally justified. They've developed myriad matrices and identified various characteristics that supposedly identify and differentiate between just and unjust wars.

Despite their considerable pontification on the subject, philosophers aren't necessarily the best judges of what makes a war just. Instead, the warrior who's actually doing the fighting will often have the better perspective. The warrior sees war with a proximity neither academics nor the media are regularly exposed to. The warrior has a unique perspective of the nature of warfare, and can be a better judge of what makes war just.

The concept of war is clearly biblical, as there are many references to it in the Scriptures. Furthermore, as we've seen in this book, we read in the Book of Exodus, "The Lord is a warrior; the Lord is His name" (Exod. 15:3). And, as noted previously, Revelation 19 describes a scene where Jesus Himself returns to the earth as a warrior, leading a great army to finally destroy His enemies.

Until Christ returns to bring His peace to all mankind, nations will continue to experience or be threatened by warfare, just as they have been from the beginning of time. So the issue continually confronts us: *When is war justified? When is it acceptable to engage in war, and when does God Himself sanction war? It is a question that will never leave us, particularly in our day of global terror. And it is a question every Christian must ask in his or her own soul. What will you do when war—spiritual or physical—comes to your home...or your homeland?*

WAR, WARFARE, AND COMBAT

In discussing the just war concept, it's essential to determine what *war* really is, and how it should be understood in our society and in the heart of a committed believer in Jesus Christ.

In his book *Morality and Global Justice* Michael Boylan defines *war* as "an aggressive act by one state against the territory or sovereignty of another state for the purposes of gaining land, resources, or strategic advantage according to internationally recognized rules and constraints governing such action." And he defines *just war theory* as "a moral account of (a) when it is morally permissible to go to war, and (b) how the war may be conducted."[1]

Another term used in discussing warfare is *combat*, a noun that can be defined as "a fight, struggle, or controversy as between two persons, teams, or ideas."[2] Combat is the action that takes place when armies square off on the field of battle, where closing with and destroying the opponent is the mission of each side. Combat is the cutting edge of warfare and the place where casualties are taken and where the ugliest part of war is seen. When a warrior is engaged in combat, he has little focus on the larger concept of war, since he's normally fighting to impose his own will on his enemy and to survive to fight another day.

War carries connotations of politics, but combat is a primal struggle between individuals who are generally organized into some form of fighting units. Carl von Clausewitz, in his famous treatise *On War*, said that "War is politics by other means."[3] But for the warrior who's fighting for his life and those of his fellow warriors, the connection between war and politics has little meaning in the heat of battle. Sometimes there are even instances of combat when there is no actual "war," declared or otherwise.

For the purpose of discussing the concept of just war, I've chosen to think of *war, warfare,* and *combat* as conditions under which warriors are engaged in a life-and-death struggle for reasons that *they* believe are just—and not simply because their governments have made that judgment. In this discussion the words *war* and *combat* are used somewhat interchangeably, since the warrior is always at the cutting edge, and he finds little distinction between the two terms.

FOR JUSTICE

In Micah 6:8 the prophet asks, "What does the LORD require of you?" The answer, he continues, is simply this: "to do justice, to love kindness, and to walk humbly with your God." That phrase *to do justice* is sometimes translated as "to do justly." In order to do justice or to act justly, one must first have a sense of justice.

The true warrior has a strong sense of justice that directs his actions. The warrior sees injustices as evil and believes that fighting against them is a noble cause, regardless of the assessments of the politicians, diplomats, and pundits. The warrior respects the decisions of those in positions of authority but still maintains an independent sense of what is *just* relative to warfare.

The true warrior cannot accept injustice when he perceives that he can reverse it, or at least believes that his actions have a chance to do so. The warrior is guided by his sense of justice, which causes him to stand apart from others in the way he thinks and the way he acts.

The true warrior is motivated by the concept of *justice*.

Unless the warrior is motivated by a sense of justice, he is little more than a mercenary. And he must believe in his cause. He must be prepared to die for it. Whether the battle is physical or spiritual, the warrior cannot function in a just manner unless he operates with a sense of justice.

The greatest warriors in God's kingdom are intercessors. They clearly fight spiritual battles out of a sense of justice. They know what they hold dear, and they are prepared to defend it at great personal cost. When a serious intercessor steps into the breach to do battle against the "powers of this dark world" (Eph. 6:12), he or she does so only after petitioning the Lord for clear guidance that this is his or her current assignment.

Whether we are intercessors or not, we must all recognize that spiritual warfare is a constant state for Christians who are doing the Lord's work—for those who have been called and have answered that call. Are we willing to spread the gospel as Jesus commanded us to do, even into dangerous parts of the world? Are we willing to support persecuted Christians around the world or stand up for the lives of unborn children? Are we willing to stand for truth even when those around us call us bigots, intolerant, or radical? Would fighting a spiritual battle over these issues be justified? What are you willing to fight and sacrifice for? Is your only concern your own welfare and spiritual condition or spiritual needs? Only a just cause can propel a Christian into spiritual battle for anything beyond his own needs and interests and sustain him throughout the fight.

Assessing Justice in America's Recent Wars

It's important that we assess the concept of just war in the daily-life context experienced by each soldier (as well that experienced by each civilian). The individual is constantly confronted with dilemmas, situations, and circumstances that could be considered war or combat on a personal level.

Many conflicts between nations derive from a formal declaration of war, but most wars simply result from one nation invading or attacking another with no official or formal announcement. The United States Congress has declared a "state of war" only five times in US history, the last time being World War II, even though US forces have been involved in major conflicts throughout its history. The conflicts in Korea and Vietnam, as well as the Gulf War of 1990–1991 and, a decade later, the military actions in Iraq and Afghanistan, were not "declared" wars in the sense that World

Wars I and II were, but they did have official support emanating from Congress.

America was drawn into World War II as a result of the devastating attack on Pearl Harbor in 1941. Few Americans questioned our nation's entry into the conflict; it was instantly deemed an issue of self-defense. The premise that we were entering a just war was easy to accept.

When the conflict in Korea began in 1950, it was clearly a just war for the South Koreans, who had been invaded by their Korean brothers to the north. But US involvement was a different matter. Many Americans weren't easily convinced that sacrificing the lives of young Americans in a war for another nation's freedom was justifiable. The same sentiments were expressed when the fighting in Vietnam escalated in the 1960s. Many Americans questioned the rationale for fighting to sustain a corrupt government in South Vietnam.

US leaders had identified critical American interests before committing our forces to combat in both places. In the prevailing view, the possibility of Communist expansion was a serious threat to the entire free world. Left unchecked, the Communist objectives of global dominance and conquest would jeopardize America's future.

Coming ashore in Pusan, Korea, in June of 1950, US soldiers saw the desperate plight of the Korean people who had been driven from their homes and villages by the murderous army from North Korea. Most realized right away that their presence and sacrifice there was justifiable, but for reasons that were different from those of the politicians.

In Vietnam, soldiers entering the hamlets and villages where the Viet Cong had brutalized the local inhabitants and robbed them of any hope for a future of self-determination knew that fighting for these people was justifiable. They were warriors with little regard for politics. Furthermore, they knew that the media and the academics had their own agenda, and that it wouldn't allow them to see the just side of the conflict.

When American tanks and armored personnel carriers rolled into Kuwait City in February of 1991, watching the cheers and tears of the Kuwaitis who had suffered at the hands of the Iraqi army for months, the fighting men and women took pride. They'd done their jobs and done them well. A nation was liberated, a people set free, an invading force expelled. America wasn't alone in this fight, but without America, this day would not have come, and Kuwait would have been permanently annexed by Saddam Hussein and his regime. And the people of Kuwait would have continued to endure the torture, rape, and pillaging from the Iraqi army. Every warrior entering the city that day knew that this was a just war and they were proud to be part of it.

The war in Iraq against the government of Saddam Hussein that began in March of 2003 brought a new dilemma for the American public, that of *preemption*. Many Americans argued that the Iraqi regime presented no threat to the United States and objected to the invasion. Some members of Congress also expressed opposition, but a majority favored a preemptive intervention into the heartland of the nation that only a few years earlier had invaded and terrorized neighboring Kuwait.

US intelligence assessed that Hussein had an arsenal of weapons of mass destruction (WMD), including a nascent nuclear program. Ultimately the WMD assessment was proven wrong, even though American forces did in fact discover large stockpiles of chemical weapons after the invasion.

When deciding whether to invade Iraq, President George W. Bush was convinced that Saddam was a threat to critical US interests in the Mideast and must be dealt with before he repeated his aggression—especially with possible weapons of mass destruction to help him accomplish his objectives.

Was this a just war based on what American leaders believed at the time? Many still argue that even if the intelligence had been accurate, there was no reasonable justification for a preemptive invasion.

To go a step further, was the attack on Iraq justifiable, based on the concept of stopping a brutal bully who terrorized his own people as well as his neighbors? Saddam Hussein killed an estimated one hundred eighty thousand Iraqi citizens in Northern Iraq when he dropped tons of chemical weapons on Kurdish villages there. Is it just to save people from such tyranny, brutality, and repression? The true warrior thinks so.

Like our warriors in Korea and Vietnam, American warriors in Iraq could recognize the evil and injustice of the situation, and knew in their souls that they could make a difference. *A just war?* I think so.

Justifying Preemption

Some believe that preemption is never justified. In their minds war cannot be justified by the preempting power for any reason. However, let's look at another case in point.

In 1967 Egypt dismissed the UN force that had been placed in the Sinai Peninsula to monitor and report aggression by either Israel or Egypt against each other. The UN troops were supposed to be a buffer between the two nations.

After dismissing those troops, Egypt began to mass its own forces along the Suez Canal and blockaded the Israeli port of Eilat. On May 30, 1967, Egypt and Jordan signed a mutual defense pact that brought Iraqi troops to Jordan the next day.

The winds of war were clearly blowing against Israel, and Israeli leaders knew it. Prime Minister Levi Eshkol and his cabinet were forced into a difficult position. Already outnumbered militarily by a wide margin, Israel's leaders had to decide whether they would (a) allow the Arab coalition to attack first and then call for US and UN assistance or (b) strike preemptively to improve their odds of defeating a superior force.

Prime Minister Eshkol chose to strike. A surprise ground and air attack against Egyptian forces was launched on the morning of June 5, and it destroyed Egypt's air force, its most lethal threat. Israel went on to victory against an Arab coalition of four primary nations with support from at least five others.

Israel's victory came at a high cost—nearly a thousand Israeli troops dead and another forty-five hundred wounded. Was this a case of justifiable preemption? Did Israel's understanding and appreciation of the threat they faced justify their attack on June 5?

The philosopher relaxing in the safety of an American university campus might opine that Israel was the aggressor and therefore not engaged in a just war. But put that same man in an apartment in the suburbs of Tel Aviv early in June 1967, and he might view things differently.

One fact is irrefutable: the Israeli military wanted to strike to reduce the threats against them and to improve their chances of winning. For them, this conflict was clearly a just war. It was a matter of national survival, and the politics of the moment meant little to them.

REMEMBERING THE BIBLICAL PICTURE

As stated earlier, war is a biblical concept. It began in the Garden of Eden when the serpent tempted Eve to eat of the forbidden fruit. That was the original example of the war between good and evil. It was spiritual warfare.

That war continues, and every warrior has a strong awareness of the realities of this underlying struggle.

Myriad wars are described in the Bible, many of which were initiated at God's direction to bring justice or to fulfill His promises to His people, the Jews. Stories of warriors and warfare are prominent in Scripture. And God routinely used warriors to do great things for His kingdom in addition to fighting wars.

God has called men to war repeatedly. Moses had to make war on the Amalekites at Rephidim as he led the Israelites out of bondage in Egypt (Exod. 17). When Joshua stood on the banks of the Jordan

River and looked into the Promised Land, he was assured by God of the victory over the enemy that was waiting for him. God exhorted him to "be strong and courageous" as he led the men of Israel into battle against the current inhabitants of the land. (See Joshua 1:1–9.)

Later Gideon was selected by God to lead three hundred men in a preemptive strike against the Midianites (Judg. 7). Even later the psalmist and mighty King David was a great warrior who fought many battles to protect the Jewish people and secure their borders. God showed him favor in war, and even called him a man after His own heart.

Those who choose to characterize Jesus as a pacifist are entitled to that view, but I for one see Jesus as the ultimate warrior who makes clear that we must fight for justice.

One especially revealing verse in this regard is Luke 22:36, where Jesus directed His disciples to arm themselves in preparation for building His church. Bible scholars have tried for centuries to explain what Jesus really meant in this verse; some insist that He was using a metaphor and didn't really mean "sell your cloak and buy a sword." But I believe He meant exactly what He said—*buy a sword.*

He wasn't directing them to build His church with the sword; He was simply communicating that in building the church, they could expect to encounter physical battles and would have to be prepared. Although their battle would be primarily spiritual, there would be times when their spiritual enemy would be manifest in a physical threat. Remember that all the disciples were eventually martyred for their faith and obedience.

Jesus was, is, and will be a warrior, and He expects His followers to be the same. But His warriors must fight for justice and to overcome evil—and never for revenge or personal gain.

Make no mistake: I am not advocating that readers should grab their AR-15s and join a militia that is bent on fighting a domestic insurgency. Our founders gave us what we need to peacefully change our culture, environment, and government. The US Constitution allows us to elect our own leaders. It is called the "consent of the governed." When I say "fight" for justice, I am referring to being willing to stand on principle. It means having the courage to stand publicly for what you believe.

How many leaders have you seen who compromise on their fundamental beliefs? Either they don't know what they believe or they lack the courage to stand for what they believe. Compromise on principles is not an option. Political correctness is the result of a lack of courage, plain and simple. So decide what you believe and think about how far you are willing to go to defend your beliefs and values. The Bible says, "If you do not stand firm in your faith, you will not stand at all" (Isa. 7:9, NIV). Does your faith matter to you? Are you willing to stand firm and defend it?

WOUNDED

It's said that you never hear the bullet that hits you. Well, that could be true, but I wasn't so sure. I was in a UH-60 Black Hawk, and the noise from the rotor blades was drowning out the guns on the ground that were shooting at us. When the .50-caliber rounds slammed into my chest and shoulder, I knew I was hit pretty hard. Pain set in quickly after a brief period of numbness, and I began to lose a substantial amount of blood.

We were still in the air over the Caribbean island of Grenada, and the battle was raging down below us as US forces invaded the island to rescue a group of American medical students and to liberate the small nation. The date was October 24, 1983. The small island was in the hands of an illegitimate government as a result of a Cuban sponsored coup d'état. The Cuban objective, acting as Soviet surrogates, was to build an airfield that would accommodate the largest Soviet bombers, thereby giving the Soviets a base from which they could strike elsewhere in North and South America.

President Ronald Reagan, a staunch anti-Communist, refused to allow the USSR to gain that kind of foothold in the Western

Hemisphere. He ordered the US Atlantic Command into action, with a directive to invade the island and return it to its rightful leaders, those who had been elected by the people of Grenada. US special operations forces were to spearhead the operation.

So here I was in the lead Black Hawk, with two gaping holes in me, watching the battle unfold. I knew I might die before I could get to a safe location and receive medical treatment. A .50-caliber bullet makes a BIG hole—and I knew how serious my injury was.

My thoughts turned to a simple question: Is this worth it? If I die here, is it worth dying for? Are we doing the right thing by invading this postage-stamp piece of soil in the Caribbean? I needed to know that my life would be sacrificed for a just cause.

Then I considered the obvious. Ronald Reagan obviously thought that committing American lives to this fight was justifiable, and that was good enough for me. Reagan was an honorable patriot, and he believed in what we were doing; after all, he sent us here. The people in Grenada had been robbed of their freedom and were being brutalized by their occupiers. The American medical students there were confined to their campus with none of the basic freedoms of a democracy. The Soviets were a known threat. We would reduce that threat and restore those liberties through our sacrifices, and free these people in a foreign land.

Yes, this *was* a just cause.

OK, that was resolved in my mind. Next question: How do I stay alive?

Miraculously I survived and made it back to the army hospital at Fort Bragg, North Carolina. My recovery would be a slow process, with much time spent in the hospital.

Meanwhile my conclusions about the just nature of the Grenada operation were confirmed as I lay in my hospital bed two days after being shot. I was watching the television news when a reporter thrust a microphone in front of an elderly lady in Grenada. She was one of those who had suffered greatly during the occupation by the Cubans and Communists. Toothless and dressed in tattered clothing, the lady looked directly into the camera, and with tears in her eyes she said, "God bless Ronald Reagan, and God bless America!"

Yes, we were in a just war—and I was honored to be part of it. My injuries suddenly seemed insignificant.

Chapter 13

THE GREATEST WARRIOR
WHO EVER LIVED

Man of the In-Between

Greater love has no one than this, that
one lay down his life for his friends.
• JESUS, IN JOHN 15:13 •

MANY YEARS AGO as a young boy in a cozy little neighborhood in central Washington state I learned a valuable lesson. We had a neighborhood bully, Jimmy C., and it seemed he would never stop throwing dirt clods and using strong-arm tactics to terrorize smaller children. Yes, we complained, protested, and begged him to be reasonable. But time after time "negotiation" failed. Nothing worked.

Until one day one of us mustered enough courage to stand up to him. Lying flat on his back, with his arm wrapped around an irrigation pipe, Jimmy experienced an amazing change of perspective. He suddenly understood the logic in leaving the little people alone.

Here's the lesson for all of us: bullies never quit—until someone takes the initiative to stand between them and their victims. Recall Goliath, or Hitler, or Saddam, or bin Laden, or the devil himself. And that's why we need warriors. Like you.

The warrior is the man of the in-between. With mind and heart committed to transcendent righteous principles, he offers himself to shield others.

MAN OF THE IN-BETWEEN

Flash back three thousand years to watch a man of the in-between in action. Envision the Valley of Elah. The armies of Philistia appear along the valley's south ridge. The northern ridge is occupied by the tribes of Israel. Both armies are motionless, as they have been for several mornings. Thousands of warriors frozen in place, listening to the roar of *the giant.*

The pride of Philistia, bully of the land, the nation's warrior champion, battle-hardened and taller and stronger than any other, this giant moves down from the southern ridgeline into the center of the valley, near a small creek running through it. He stands in the in-between.

With a voice like thunder, he taunts the terrified troops on the north ridge. His challenge is simple: "Step up, you cowards. Select your own champion, and let the two of us meet here in the in-between. The last man standing will carry the day for his nation, and this war will be over."

But on the north ridge, no one moves. The challenge goes unheeded. No one will face the giant, and no one will volunteer to be the man of the in-between.

King Saul himself, Israel's then version of a champion, head and shoulders above his own people, has no heart for the in-between.

But Jesse's kid does.

From the far edge of the north ridge, a solitary voice breaks the silence. A youngster's voice. He's an errand boy, not even a soldier. His mother has sent him here merely to carry a bag of cheese sandwiches to his older brothers who serve in the army.

But there's something about the voice. It's intense. This boy is incensed by the lack of response from Israel's army. David *shouts—* to any who'll hear—that he's willing to be the man of the in-between.

To this boy from Bethlehem, it's a straightforward proposition. The bully is out of order. For the good of others that bully has to be stopped in his tracks.

Packing his simple shepherd's gear, David voluntarily steps between his countrymen and all that would harm them.

And you know the story. The boy stood tall that day, the giant lost his head, and the Philistines, shocked and sullen, abandoned the field.

DAVID'S SON

David was a warrior, a man of the in-between. Is it any wonder, then, that a thousand years after that shoot-out at Elah, the New Testament opens with these words: "The book of the generation of Jesus Christ, *the son of David*" (Matt. 1:1, KJV)?

Get the picture? Jesus, King of the universe, born in the city of David, is so pleased to be identified with David that the Spirit of God introduces Him, on page one of the New Testament, as the greater Son of David.

What was it about David that Jesus valued? Probably multiple things. But certainly one thing heads the list—in the Old Testament, in 1 Samuel 13:14, God introduced David to us as "a man after His own heart."

Certainly another thing Jesus valued about David was his fearless and self-sacrificial initiative at Elah. Jesus didn't fear battle. Jesus was a warrior. As we've noted before, the first hint of Him in Scripture, in the first book of the Bible, describes Him from the get-go as a warrior—a wounded warrior, no less. In Genesis the Old Testament introduces Messiah as one who will be wounded by the enemy of our souls, the devil himself. And it informs us that in this hand-to-hand combat between the Messiah and our old adversary, Satan himself, the Messiah will deal a mortal wound to the devil (Gen. 3:15). That Genesis account refers, of course, to the fight that would take place millennia later on a hill called Calvary.

A thousand years after David met the giant, the greater Son of David met the giant of giants, the dark one, Satan himself. Jesus demonstrated the warrior soul when He climbed that piece of high ground called Calvary and faced off with the champion of evil, the bully of all bullies. Warrior that He is, Christ stood between us and all that would destroy us. Jesus deliberately took the full fury of the enemy. He intentionally took the wounds, absorbed the blows, and shed His own blood for the rest of us.

He is truly the greatest warrior ever.

Think about it. That combat on Calvary is what secured the ultimate victory at the end of the ages. The blood that was shed that day provided the victory of victories. That's why Christians preach and sing so robustly about "the power in the blood" and the "victory at the cross."

Calvary finds something of a parallel in D-Day, June 6, 1944. Much like the fighting on Omaha Beach determined the final outcome of World War II a year later, so the battle on the cross at Calvary secured the ultimate victory in the war that will actually end all wars, at the end of time.

Further—just as it was with D-Day—though the ultimate victory has been secured, the battles aren't yet over. Our Savior locked in the victory at Calvary two thousand years ago, but His days in battle are not finished. On a day still future, the Son of David will don a blood-spattered robe, summon His army of saints, mount a great white war horse, and take up His sword. Then (and only then) will there be peace and safety on our battered planet.

In the meantime, as Jesus said, we "hear continually of wars and rumors of war." That's why you're a soldier today. There's a high and honored place for the warrior, both in Christian theology and in this constitutional republic, the United States of America.

So Very Real

But back to the greater Son of David. As a warrior, where do you go to look for the ideal warrior model? Does history reveal one warrior who stands above them all?

Indeed! The answer is clear: Jesus is the greatest warrior who ever lived.

But then, why is it that if anyone asked us to picture the archetypal warrior, the classic standard of the soldier, the image entering our minds is *not* one of Jesus? Why is that?

I have to confess that for many years I wouldn't have pictured Jesus as the greatest of warriors. That simply wouldn't have occurred to me. The picture of Jesus painted for me in childhood Sunday school was that of a kind person, gentle, sweet, caring, loving. And that's all true about Jesus (as it should be about every soldier). But Jesus was certainly never portrayed as a warrior to us kids.

Have we then missed something important?

I think so. That picture of Jesus on the Sunday school flannelgraphs was most often incomplete. Likewise, the picture of Jesus commonly portrayed in our culture, in movies and books, is usually distorted as well. I believe we've allowed our vision of Jesus to become clouded, and actually twisted to distortion by a popular media that at the very least misunderstands Jesus—if not hates Him outright.

Let me quote here from *Tender Warrior:*

> Even the single most famous portrait of Jesus makes Him look more like a pouting model for herbal shampoo than a man. Doesn't it? Really. His eyes aren't toward you. The face is thin and aloof. The long hair is waved and feminine.[1]

Hollywood seems to consistently portray Jesus Christ as some kind of space cadet. His eyes are never quite focused. His mind is never quite engaged with reality. He's different to the point of weird. He's always halfway between here and somewhere else. His mysticism is so spooky and otherworldly that He can't be real. The portrayal seems unreal to us. So we subconsciously relegate Him to irrelevance.

That is most decidedly *not* the Jesus of the Bible. Somehow we've allowed Him to be painted as "gentle Jesus, meek and mild" or "the pale Galilean." He's so much more than those images. *He is very real.* Forever relevant. And, if I read the Bible correctly, fully human.

And Then There's "the Church"

If you've had a negative experience with "the church," welcome to the club! Sometimes "church" can seem like a one-word description for all that is wrong with Christians. But if you've had a bad experience with Christians somewhere along the line, don't let that stop you from getting to know Jesus Christ! Someone once said, "There would be more Christians in this world if it wasn't for us Christians." *Ouch.*

I tend to agree with another similar sentiment: "Christ's reputation has been done more harm by His friends than His enemies." And then when you stir a little Christian television, so-called, into the formula, it's something of a minor miracle that people still have any inclination at all to pursue getting to know Jesus.

I want to let you in on a little secret that has sustained me for decades—don't draw your picture of Jesus from the odd caricatures that abound among His followers. Rather, take Him at His Word. Find Him in the Bible. That's where He is most clearly made known.

As a child, I grew up in the church. I saw all the goofy arguments over carpet color and communion cups. You know what I mean. So I chucked it. Walked away from church, from Christians, and from any notion there actually was a God who took people seriously. I wandered in a wilderness of my own making for several years in the 1960s. But over time almighty God Himself convinced me to find Him—the *real* Him—not in those crazy caricatures often represented by His less-than-mature followers, but in the pages of Scripture.

There—in the Bible and only in the Bible—were "ancient words, ever true," transcending time and culture, and every foolish mis-representation. God's Word burst through the walls I had erected. The Bible, like a mighty, immovable anvil, withstood the blows of every hammer I could muster. I yielded my soul and my life to Jesus. Change began to show itself. Slowly, surely, steadily, Christ proved Himself to be everything He said He is—Savior, Lord, and coming King.

As an adult, I pastored a church for more than thirty years. I've pretty much seen it all. Goofy arguments, pettiness, immaturity, incoherent thinking, bizarre choices, striking small-mindedness—all "in the name of Jesus." I've seen the Bible so badly abused by Christians that there was nothing left to do but laugh. It's axiomatic—people regularly mangle the Bible, misinterpreting it for their own purposes.

So here's the bottom line: in your search for ultimate truth don't allow your personal experience with people to be your final authority. Let Christ speak for Himself. And that's precisely what He does in the Bible. Over the years I have often had to remind myself—don't take your picture of the church from what you see around you. Rather, form your perspective of the church from what Jesus says about it. After all, Christ loves His church, died for her, and sees in her silliness and shortcomings that bride who will one day be fully transformed and without blemish. (See Ephesians 5:25–27.)

Today the church often seems, as one writer described her, to be something of a Cinderella with amnesia, hideous among the ashes but destined for glory! Look straight at Jesus Christ, revealed in Scripture, and don't let yourself be misguided by any of His well-intentioned but sorrowfully lacking "witnesses." You'll find Jesus to be more manly, more godly, more truthful, and more winsome than you've been able so far to imagine.

No, Jesus is no shampoo model. He's no Sunday school puppet. And He's certainly not some spooky, spacey spiritual weirdo. He is Jesus! The Christ! Strong. Straight up. Smart as a whip. And no-nonsense about spiritual reality and your eternal life. Jesus Christ is fully God and delightfully human.

Are you sure you know Him? Personally? Some of America's church buildings are full of people who call themselves Christians, but don't know Him personally and therefore are not genuinely saved people. Just to be sure for yourself—that you know He died for *you* personally—let's look at Him a little closer.

Hangin' on Your Cross

I've taken a liking to Toby Keith's rendition of "If I Was Jesus." It's worth your time to pick up a copy. Seriously. The one song is worth the price of the whole CD. Fittingly enough, it's on Toby's *Shock'n Y'all* album. Yes, it would likely be something of a shock to some of the silver-haired church ladies. (By the way, equally fitting, the same album includes the song "American Soldier.") Of course, you need the music to appreciate the song, but Toby's fundamental point is well taken.[2]

Jesus didn't come to the high and mighty—and He really didn't relate well to the "religious" people of His day. He pretty much hung out with the wrong crowd and had a good time with the "regular folks." In fact, sometimes He was the life of the party, as He was at the wedding where He turned water into wine. And here is the big point: although Jesus knows everything about every one of us—including the nasty details of the rotten dark side in all our hearts—He hung on the cross for us anyway!

The point is, Jesus was real. He was a man. Sinless, to be sure, but tempted in every way all the rest of us are. And He absolutely loved "little" people, like most folks are. Though He was truly "high and mighty" in the ultimate sense, He was also very much down to earth. He didn't strut. He humbled himself, completely, to walk in our shoes.

Jesus was a blue-collar carpenter. I expect He had heavily callused hands. And in His day carpenters didn't go to Home Depot for lumber; they climbed the hills, cut the trees, and dragged or carried the wood back to the shop. And they built with stone as well. Visualize the heavy mallet and the massive chisel. I expect Jesus had some major forearms and a set of "guns" between His elbows and shoulders.

Jesus is compassionate and personable and perceptive, but He's also strong, focused, mission-driven, and forceful. He's no Casper the Friendly Ghost. He's incredibly alive, very much in touch, and incredibly powerful.

TAKE A LOOK

My visual picture of Jesus changed dramatically when I visited Israel many years ago. Here's a little more from *Tender Warrior*:

> The shampoo ads fell off my mental screen when we stepped off the plane and met David (pronounced Dah-VEED), the driver for our group. I watched David for nine weeks. He was a twenty-five-year-old Jewish male in his prime, a native-born *sabra*. That's the modern Hebrew term for a prickly pear cactus: tough on the outside, tender and sweet within. David's skin was dark. Dark by pigment, dark by the bronzing of the sun. His hair was black, medium length, somewhat wavy. It hung naturally on his head and matted on his forehead in the afternoon heat.
>
> More than anything else, I noticed his eyes. Very dark. Sometimes hard as black steel, sometimes soft, with smiles dancing on the edges. Piercing eyes. Kind eyes. Intelligent eyes. Eyes brimming with life.
>
> David was so serious and so hilarious all at the same time that we were irresistibly drawn to him. He had just been released from the hospital, where he had been convalescing

from wounds suffered in the (1973) Yom Kippur War. I'll never forget the picture he made as he first stood before us—clad in neat khakis, arms folded, legs apart, smiling a welcome. In love with life, in love with his family, in love with his people and his nation.[3]

David was strong. He was reflective. He exuded that intangible draw of a leader. And he was passionate—something like an Israeli Tim Tebow. He just kept it up, a steady, relentless high performance, defying normal descriptions.

With this exceptional specimen of Hebrew manhood standing before us, you can understand how readily the tape in my mind rewound back through three thousand years to that first *Dah-VEED*, from the same Hebrew gene pool. I half expected our bronzed driver to recite, in a strong, sonorous voice, a psalm from the first David. That first David was the consummate Israeli man of his day. He defined Hebrew manhood.

My mind fast-forwarded from the Iron Age to the opening of the New Testament and to the greater Son of David, the consummate Man of all the Ages.

See Jesus. Take a good long look. Look straight at Him. See Him accurately. Always a king. Never a victim. Even that horrible day on the cross, when He sacrificed His life for the rest of us, it was all on *His* terms, not the enemy's. He's the only human to have ever died actively. All the rest of us are necessarily passive and helpless before death's insidious coming. It takes us, whether we want it or not. Not so with Jesus. He's the only human to have ever actively dismissed His own spirit. When the God-Man hung on that cross and finished His sacrificial mission, the Bible tells us He shouted out loud, with a strong voice, "It is finished!" (See John 19:28–30.)

I believe that was no whimper.

It was no sigh of resignation.

I believe *it was a shout of pure triumph.* The ultimate victory was secured!

That loud voice proclaimed victory so strongly that it shook the cosmos from the dungeons of hell to the corona of Alpha Centauri. The warrior soul of the greatest warrior ever had seized the challenge. He had taken the objective. He'd carried the day. He had paid the ultimate price. The war's outcome was secured.

THE TRUTH DAWNS

So here's the point. When you're overwhelmed in life's battles, whether in the heat of a firefight or the pain of a soulish wound, run to Jesus for strength. David did. Over and over again. Time after time David took his soul in his hands and ran to God for help.

One of the things I love most about that Iron Age warrior is his transparency. Real men are like that. They know themselves, warts and all. They're not afraid to face their own weaknesses openly. It's not that great warriors know no fear; it's that they stare it down with purpose and courage.

David faced himself and his fears regularly. Let's look back again at one such occasion we've examined, a time when David found himself commanding what might be called a battalion light—about four hundred infantrymen in this case. They were in trouble, holed up in a cave in the wilderness. They were not happy campers. In fact, Scripture says (1 Sam. 22) they were flat discouraged, depressed, and beat up. And David was no exception. In his own after-action report he described what was going on in his own warrior soul. And it wasn't pretty. At first.

That report is called Psalm 142, the psalm we explored earlier in our discussion of unflagging optimism and quiet confidence. Recall the words:

> I cry aloud [*a guttural cry*] with my voice to the LORD; I make supplication [*beg*] with my voice to the LORD. I pour out [*bitterly vomit*] my complaint before Him; I declare [*slowly and*

deliberately] my trouble before Him. When my spirit was overwhelmed within me... [But wait!] You knew my path.

—PSALM 142:1–3

David realizes God knows perfectly well what he's facing—and this rights his spirit:

You are my refuge....Bring my soul out of prison, so that I may give thanks to Your name; the righteous will surround me, for You will deal bountifully with me.

—PSALM 142:5–7

Under enormous pressure David's equilibrium is seriously bruised, his perspective skewed. He can't take it anymore. In painfully transparent conversation with God David bears his soul, openly admitting his pain and fear.

In the midst of his prayerful authenticity it dawns on him who he's talking to. "Whoa, wait a minute; You're God! You already know!" That simple realization ("The sovereign God knows what I'm facing; how could I forget that?") brings strength to David's soul. He begins to develop a spiritual momentum that bolsters his confidence.

He ends his prayer with a fresh tone of optimism: *The day's coming when I'll stand before good people and tell them just how faithful You are. For You always deal graciously with Your people* (my paraphrase of verse 7).

David realized what every Christian learns eventually: there's no place you can go—no place so dark, so despairing, so discouraging, so depressing—where God is not with you. It's true wherever you are—whether you're painting parking stripes on a stateside post, or pulling a trigger in the mountains of Afghanistan.

You see, David *knew* God. He had a personal, believing relationship with Him.

How about you? Let me ask again: Do you know this God?

Personally? Have you placed your complete trust in Him? This is the single most important issue of your life. Forever.

True or False?

It just so happens that the God to whom David prays is Jesus Himself! Jesus is God Almighty in the flesh. The New Testament insists upon that.

It's what was revealed to John the Apostle when he walked beside Jesus. In one part of the Gospel of John we find John commenting on how so many people still didn't believe in Jesus, even after seeing the miraculous signs He performed. John then quotes words from the prophet Isaiah about blinded eyes and hardened hearts.

One of the passages John quotes is from Isaiah 6—maybe the most potent description of the Almighty in the Old Testament. Here Isaiah, prince of prophets, describes God on the throne in the temple of heaven itself. Isaiah says he "saw the Lord sitting on a throne, lofty and exalted," with the train of His robe billowing out to fill heaven's temple, and angels hovering about Him (v. 1). Seeing this, Isaiah felt the temple foundations trembling as the voice of God called out while smoke filled the temple (v. 4).

In the New Testament John explains for us that the awesomely powerful and majestic One whom Isaiah saw sitting on that throne is *none other than Jesus Himself!* John declares, "Isaiah was referring to Jesus when he said this, because he saw the future and spoke of the Messiah's glory" (John 12:41, NLT).

Let's be straight up here—*Jesus Christ is the almighty God of Scripture!* And He knew it. He said the kinds of things about Himself no mere human being can or should ever say. In fact, if anyone else said the things Jesus said, we'd give him a free white jacket and lock him up in a padded cell.

Let's take another look at the fact that there's no wiggle room with Jesus. Either He is who He said He is, or He's nothing at all. There's no third alternative: He's either telling the truth or not.

Jesus spoke things such as this: "I say to you, before Abraham was, I AM" (John 8:58, ESV). Jesus was declaring that He predated Abraham, who had lived two thousand years earlier. Jesus was claiming to be eternally alive—God Himself. And His audience understood precisely what He meant.

It's an incredible claim. Either true. Or false.

On another occasion, staring a funeral service in the face, Jesus made it clear that death was no big deal, certainly not terminal. He said, "I am the resurrection and the life. Anyone who believes in me will live, even after dying. Everyone who lives in me and believes in me will never ever die" (John 11:25–26, NLT). Jesus claimed to have complete power over death.

Again, it's an incredible claim. *True. Or false.*

Jesus made numerous other outrageous claims, all of which beg the ultimate question: *Is He who He claimed to be? Or is He not?*

Someone summarized the issue this way: Jesus was either right or wrong. He was either God or He wasn't. And you can't call Him a great teacher if He was wrong. Great teachers don't say the kind of things Jesus said—unless those claims are true.

Jesus just doesn't allow us any wiggle room. Only one of these things is true:

1. If He was wrong and didn't know it, He's merely a fool.

2. If He was wrong and knew it, He's just one more charlatan.

3. Or if He's was right, He is God Almighty Himself!

C. S. Lewis called it accurately: Jesus is either a lunatic, a liar, or the Lord Himself.[4] And that's the fundamental point of this book—Jesus is precisely who He claimed to be, the ultimate transcendent cause. Jesus is the Alpha and Omega, the beginning and the end. Everything begins and ends with Jesus.

So where do you stand with Jesus? Who do you believe He is? Your eternity rests in your answer. Do you *know* Jesus?

KNOWING HIM

Listen up now. If you want your life to count, you need to know Jesus. If you want to live forever, you need to belong to Christ. This is the biggest single point of this entire book. Do *you* know God? Do you *know* Him? Do you know the real *Him?* Personally? Do you have a truly personal relationship with Him?

It's possible for you to *know* Jesus! You can call upon Him in the midst of battle just as David did. But only if you know Him personally.

That begs the question: *How do I get to know Him?*

Glad you asked. Let me introduce you.

Let me do it by sharing a story from my own past. As I've mentioned, I spent my childhood in a tiny coal-mining town tucked away in the mountains of Washington state. Until I left home for college, I'd never traveled east of Idaho.

The best part about college for me was getting to know people who became lifelong friends. One of them was a teammate from Massachusetts. He was from a prominent New England family with significant connections to Harvard, to Boston's financial centers, and to some of America's biggest business corporations. They were direct descendants of more than one passenger on the *Mayflower.* Their historic old home, dating from the early 1700s, was an American treasure. Some of the furnishings were from the earliest days of our nation's history, predating the American Revolution by decades.

And to top it off, every member of the family was kind and generous, unselfish and humble. As far as I was concerned, this family was as close to American royalty as it gets.

During breaks from college classes, I traveled to their home, ate their food, slept in their beds, and lived like one of their own sons.

Here's a question for you: How in the world did a coal miner's kid from the boonies (who didn't even know the name of his own great-grandfather at the time) come to be treated like a son by such a special and historic family?

The answer is pretty simple—I had a personal relationship with their son. Their son was my ticket into that home and family. He'd invited me home, and I'd accepted.

The same is true of my home in heaven. *I know the Son.* Because of a personal relationship with Jesus, the heavenly Father invites me to live with them. Forever!

There's only one way to live forever, only one way to get into heaven, only one way to relate to God—and that's through the Son. Jesus Himself said it clearly: "I am the way, the truth, and the life" (John 14:6, KJV). In another place God's Word says, "There is salvation in no one else; for there is no other name under heaven that has been given among men by which we must be saved" (Acts 4:12). The only way we sinful earthlings will ever live eternally in heaven is through a personal relationship with Jesus Christ.

THE BASICS

God's Word describes a couple basic steps for coming to know Jesus and accepting the Son's invitation home:

1. You must believe *Jesus is who He said He is*—the perfect Son of God who died on the cross to pay the penalty for our sins, and who rose again from the dead on the third day.

If you confess with your mouth that Jesus is Lord and believe in your heart that God raised him from the dead, you will be saved.

—ROMANS 10:9, ESV

2. You must believe *you* are who Jesus said *you* are—a sinner who cannot live up to God's standard of perfection and therefore worthy of death.

All have sinned and fall short of the glory of God.

—Romans 3:23

The wages of sin is death, but the free gift of God is eternal life in Christ Jesus our Lord.

—Romans 6:23

3. You must believe these things *personally*, in mind and heart (not just with mental assent), and you must depend on Christ alone as your *only* source of salvation.

There is salvation in no one else; for there is no other name under heaven that has been given among men by which we must be saved.

—Acts 4:12

By grace you have been saved through faith; and that not of yourselves, it is the gift of God; not as a result of works, so that no one may boast.

—Ephesians 2:8–9

Whoever will call on the name of the Lord will be saved.

—Romans 10:13

If you've never accepted Jesus as your Savior, do it now. Don't think it's hard to talk to God about this or that you have to say all the right words. Don't fret over your lack of experience in praying.

A good friend of mine, near death in an army field hospital unit in Pleiku, Vietnam, was asked by a chaplain if he wanted to pray. My friend said he didn't know how. The wise chaplain said simply, "That's OK. God is a really good listener."

His point is well taken. God listens past our words and reads our heart. So don't worry about perfect vocabulary. God knows genuine repentance and faith when He sees it.

So do it now. What could possibly keep you from accepting such a gracious offer and eternal gift?

And if you've just prayed to receive Christ as your Savior, please do yourself a favor and tell a mature Christian. You need someone to help you grow in your new life in Christ. Get linked up with genuine brothers in Christ as soon as possible.

And, hey—if you've just accepted Christ in these most recent moments, let me be the first to say, "Welcome home!" Welcome to the heavenly home prepared for you by Jesus. Welcome to the fraternity of warriors before you, like Caleb, who have known and followed Him. Welcome to the ultimate transcendent cause, to an eternal life in Christ, and to a new lifestyle.

When you belong to Christ, you're guaranteed a future in the world to come. When Jesus puts on that blood-spattered robe and mounts that white war horse, and brings the world and time to its God-intended conclusion—in the moment, if you know Jesus, *you'll be riding with Him*! And you'll live forever with Him on a brand-new planet. This old planet Earth—today's war-torn, painful fight site—will be made over altogether. No more pain. No more disappointment. No more war.

You'll be at home with the Prince of Peace. How utterly and eternally sweet!

> For God so loved the world, that he gave his only Son, that whoever believes in him should not perish but have eternal life.
> —JOHN 3:16, ESV

☆ Notes ☆

EPIGRAPH

1. Rudyard Kipling, *The Works of Rudyard Kipling*, "Volume 1 Departmental Diddies and Other Versers," Project Gutenberg, http://www
.gutenberg.org/files/2334/2334-h/2334-h.htm (accessed June 18, 2014).

AN IMPORTANT NOTE TO READERS

1. *Merriam-Webster's Collegiate Dictionary*, eleventh edition (Springfield, MA: Merriam-Webster Inc., 2003), s.v., "warrior."

CHAPTER 1
THE ORIGINAL UNCLE SAM

1. George C. Marshall, Nobel Peace Prize Speech 1953, http://www
.nobelprize.org/nobel_prizes/peace/laureates/1953/press.html?print=1#
.U6ML8XJdU4I (accessed June 19, 2014).

2. Hugh Percy, Duke of Northumberland, *Letters of Hugh, Earl Percy, from Boston and New York, 1774–1776*, Charles Knowles Bolton, ed. (Boston: Goodspeed, 1902), 52–53.

3. NRA Life of Duty TV, "A Tribute to Adam Brown," http://www
.nralifeofduty.tv/patriot-profiles/video/a-tribute-to-adam-brown/list/a
-tribute-to-adam-brown (accessed June 19, 2014).

4. Video of interview, http://www.youtube.com/watch?v=28FxtSSMIwA (accessed September 18, 2014); partial video clip, transcript, and summary article also at Scott Trump, "Navy SEAL's Widow: 'We Were Blessed to Be Together,'" http://today.msnbc.msn.com/id/44056945/ns/today-today_
people/t/navy-seals-widow-we-were-blessed-be-together/ (accessed September 18, 2014).

5. Samuel Whittemore's story is taken from these sources: an account of his life by his descendant T. J. Whittemore, as included in Benjamin Cutter and William R. Cutter's *History of the Town of Arlington, Massachusetts* (Boston: David Clapp & Son, 1880), 76–77; Patrick J. Leonard, "A Veteran Long Before the War for Independence, Sam Whittemore Was America's Oldest, Bravest Soldier," http://dwhitmore.thewhitmorefamily.com/internet/
samwhit.htm (accessed September 18, 2014); Donald M. Doran, "Never Too Old: The Story of Captain Samuel Whittemore," http://www
.revolutionarywararchives.org/whittemore.html (accessed September 18, 2014); and information provided by the Sharpshooters for Liberty, http://
www.sharpshootersforliberty.org/Whittmore.htm (accessed September 18, 2014).

6. Leonard, "A Veteran Long Before the War for Independence, Sam Whittemore Was America's Oldest, Bravest Soldier."

7. Ibid.

8. Ibid.

9. Ibid.

10. Ibid.

11. Ibid.

CHAPTER 2
LIFE IS A BATTLE, EARTH IS A WAR ZONE

1. Sun Tzu, *The Art of War* (New York: Random House, 2002).

2. Stu Weber, *Spirit Warriors* (Eugene, OR: Multnomah, 2003), 19.

3. Cormac McCarthy, *Blood Meridian* (New York: Random House, 1985), 248.

4. Augustine, in *The City of God*: "The city…makes war in order to attain to this peace"; Book XV, chapter 4; "Even they who make war desire nothing but victory—desire, that is to say, to attain to peace with glory. For what else is victory than the conquest of those who resist us? And when this is done there is peace. It is therefore with the desire for peace that wars are waged, even by those who take pleasure in exercising their war-like nature in command and battle." Augustine's *The City of God*, trans. by Marcus Dods (Chicago: University of Chicago, 1952), 458, 586.

5. Weber, *Spirit Warriors*, 24–25.

6. Victor Hanson, *The Soul of Battle* (New York: Anchor Books, 2001), dust cover.

7. Ibid.

8. Ibid.

9. Cliff Graham, *Day of War* (Grand Rapids, MI: Zondervan, 2009), Note to the Reader.

10. Ibid.

11. Declaration of Independence, for complete transcript see http://www.archives.gov/exhibits/charters/declaration_transcript.html (accessed June 20, 2014).

12. Attributed to Napoleon by Maturin M. Ballou, *Treasury of Thought: Forming an Encyclopedia of Quotations from Ancient and Modern Authors* (Boston: Osgood and Co., 1872), 407.

13. Strategic Studies Institute of the US Army War College, *Why They Fight: Combat Motivation in the Iraq War*, http://www.strategicstudies institute.army.mil/pdffiles/pub179.pdf (accessed June 20, 2014), 17–18.

CHAPTER 3
GETTING A GRIP ON THE WARRIOR SOUL

1. George S. Patton, Jr., "The Secret of Victory," in *Military Essays and Articles*, ed. Charles M. Province, 297–307 (San Diego, CA: The George S. Patton, Jr. Historical Society, 2002), 303, http://www.pattonhq.com/pdffiles/vintagetext.pdf (accessed June 20, 2014).

2. As quoted in Rick Atkinson *An Army at Dawn* (New York: Henry Holt & Co., 2002).

3. Ralph J. Hall, "Slacker, Think It Over," *Songs From the Trenches*, ed. Herbert Adams Gibbons (New York: Harper & Brothers, 1893 and 1918), 67–68.

4. Eric Metaxas, *Bonhoeffer: Pastor, Martyr, Prophet, Spy* (Nashville: Thomas Nelson, 2010), back cover.

5. As quoted by Major Edwin N. McClellan, USMC, "The Meuse-Argonne Offensive," in *The United States Navy in the World War* by James Clayton Russell and William Emmet Moore (Washington, DC: US government publication, 1921), 299.

6. From the musical adaptation of Psalm 144 by Michael A. Schmid, © 2010 by Michael A. Schmid c/o True Vine Music. Napa, CA. www.truevinemusic.com. All rights reserved. Used by permission.

7. US Army, "Comprehensive Soldier Fitness: Strong Minds, Strong Bodies," October 1, 2009, http://www.army.mil/article/28194/Comprehensive_Soldier_Fitness___Strong_Minds__Strong_Bodies/ (accessed July 25, 2014).

8. Nancy Rasmussen, "Countering Impact of Persistent Conflict through Holistic Fitness," US Army, December 29, 2009, http://www.army.mil/article/32375/http://csf.army.mil/ (accessed September 18, 2014).

9. US Army, "IMCOM Pacific Region Resiliency," http://www.imcom.pac.army.mil/about/Resiliency.aspx (accessed July 25, 2014).

10. Army Sgt. Cashmere C. Jefferson, "Building Resilience Across USARPAC," February 18, 2011, http://www.army.mil/article/52143/building-resilience-across-usarpac/ (accessed July 25, 2014).

11. General Marshall spoke these words in an address at Trinity College in Connecticut in 1941. A dozen years later, when Marshall received the 1953 Nobel Peace Prize, this address was quoted at length by the presenter of the prize, Carl Joachim Hambro, at the presentation ceremony. The official website of the Nobel Prize quotes the words at http://www.nobelprize.org/nobel_prizes/peace/laureates/1953/press.html#not_7, and cites H. A. de Weerd, *Selected Speeches and Statements of General of the Army George C. Marshall*, 121–125.

CHAPTER 4
FIVE CORE REALITIES

1. Hanson, *The Soul of Battle*; quote viewed at https://www.nytimes
.com/books/first/h/hanson-battle.html (accessed June 20, 2014).

2. Rasmussen, "Countering Impact of Persistent Conflict Through Holistic Fitness."

3. US Army "IMCOM Pacific Region Resiliency"; Comprehensive Soldier & Family Fitness, http://csf2.army.mil/ (accessed July 25, 2014).

4. As quoted by Lt. Col. G. F. R. Henderson, *Stonewall Jackson and the American Civil War,* vol. 1 (London: Longmans, Green, and Co., 1898), 200.

5. Dr. Hunter McGuire, "Account of the Wounding and Death of Stonewall Jackson," published in the *Richmond Medical Journal,* May 1866; as included in Hunter McGuire and George L. Christian, *The Confederate Cause and Conduct in the War Between the States* (Richmond, VA: L. H. Jenkins, 1907), 229.

6. See John Clifford, "The Anvil of God's Word," http://www
.wholesomewords.org/poetry/bible.html (accessed July 17, 2014).

7. Søren Kierkegaard, Quotes, Encyclopedia Britannica, http://www
.britannica.com/topic/317503/supplemental-information (accessed July 17, 2014).

CHAPTER 5
A TRANSCENDENT CAUSE

1. National World War II Memorial Inscriptions, http://www
.wwiimemorial.com/archives/factsheets/inscriptions.htm (accessed July 17, 2014).

2. My friend uses these three, but perhaps he borrowed them from Harry R. Jackson, who recounted this process in his book *The Way of the Warrior* (Grand Rapids, Michigan: Chosen Books, 2005), 28–31.

3. Lt. Gen. A. A. Vandegrift, "Religion on Guadalcanal," in *Faith of Our Fighters,* ed. Chaplain Ellwood C. Nance (St. Louis: Bethany Press, 1944), 242.

4. Stephen Mansfield, *Faith of the American Soldier* (Lake Mary, FL: FrontLine, 2005), 39.

5. Winston Churchill, *My Early Life* (New York: Charles Scribner's Sons, 1930), 276.

6. Douglas MacArthur, in address given May 12, 1962, at West Point, New York. Transcribed text at http://www.americanrhetoric.com/speeches/douglasmacarthurthayeraward.html (accessed September 18, 2014).

7. Stephen Ambrose, *The Victors: Eisenhower and His Boys: The Men of World War II* (New York: Simon & Schuster, 1998), 351.

8. General Marshall spoke these words in an address at Trinity College in Connecticut in 1941. A dozen years later, when Marshall received the 1953 Nobel Peace Prize, this address was quoted at length by the presenter of the prize, Carl Joachim Hambro, at the presentation ceremony. The official website of the Nobel Prize quotes the words at http://www.nobelprize .org/nobel_prizes/peace/laureates/1953/press.html#not_7, and cites H. A. de Weerd, *Selected Speeches and Statements of General of the Army George C. Marshall*, 121–125.

9. Karl Marlantes, *What It Is Like to Go to War* (New York: Atlantic Monthly Press, 2011), 144.

10. Ibid., xi.

11. Ibid., 3–4.

12. Ibid., 7.

13. Ibid., 7–8.

14. Ibid., 8.

15. Ibid., 44.

16. Ibid., 45.

17. C. S. Lewis, *Mere Christianity* (New York: William Collins Sons, 1952), 40–41.

18. Ernest Becker, *The Denial of Death* (New York: Free Press, 1973), 6.

19. Steven Pressfield, *Gates of Fire* (New York: Doubleday, 1998), 35.

20. United States Military Academy, "Cadet Prayer," http://www.usma .edu/chaplain/sitepages/cadet%20prayer.aspx (accessed July 17, 2014).

21. As quoted in Don M. Snider, ed., *The Warrior's Character* (New York: McGraw-Hill, 2013), xvi.

22. Don Snider, *Forging the Warrior's Character: Moral Precepts from the Cadet Prayer* (Indianapolis: Learning Solutions, 2007). The author is a professor of political science at West Point, and has been a member of the academy's civilian faculty since 1990.

23. As quoted in Snider, *The Warrior's Character*, x.

24. US Army, "The Army Values," http://www.army.mil/values/ (accessed July 17, 2014).

25. Declaration of Independence, http://www.archives.gov/exhibits/ charters/declaration_transcript.html (accessed July 17, 2014).

CHAPTER 6
A SETTLED MEMORY

1. Original source unknown.

2. Stu Weber, *Infinite Impact* (Carol Stream, IL: Tyndale House Publishers, 2008), 31–37.

3. Rod Gragg, *By the Hand of Providence: How Faith Shaped the American Revolution* (New York: Simon & Schuster, 2010), 83.

4. As quoted by Patrick J. Buchanan in *The Death of the West: How Dying Populations and Immigrant Invasions Imperil Our Country and Civilization* (New York: Thomas Dunne Books, 2002), 147.

5. *The Lion King*, directed by Roger Allers and Rob Minkoff (Hollywood, CA: Walt Disney Pictures, 1995), DVD.

6. George Washington, letter to General John Armstrong, March 11, 1792, as given in *The Writings of George Washington*, vol. XII, ed. Jared Sparks (Boston: John B. Russell, 1837), 403.

7. John Adams, recorded as "notes for an oration at Braintree," as quoted by David McCullough in *John Adams* (New York: Simon and Schuster, 2001), 70.

8. As quoted by Richard Beeman in *Plain, Honest Men: The Making of the American Constitution* (New York: Random House, 2009), 412; citing ed. Max Farrand, *The Records of the Federal Convention of 1787*, rev. ed. (New Haven, Connecticut: Yale University Press, 1937, repr. 1966), vol. 3, 85.

9. Virginia Declaration of Rights, Article 15, June 12, 1776, http://www.themoralliberal.com/2012/02/16/firm-morals-frequent-recurrence-to-fundamentals-freedom/ (accessed July 18, 2014).

10. As quoted in Karel Montor, *Naval Leadership: Voices of Experience* (Annapolis, MD: United States Naval Institute, 1998), 157.

11. As relayed to the authors.

12. US Army, "The Army Values," http://www.army.mil/values/ (accessed July 18, 2014).

13. John Adams letter of October 11, 1798, as quoted in David Barton, "America Distinctively Christian," in *Christian America? Perspectives on Our Religious Heritage*, ed. Daryl C. Cornett (Nashville: B&H Publishing, 2011), 31; citing *The Works of John Adams*, ed. C. F. Adams (Boston: Charles C. Little and James Brown, 1851), vol. IX, 229.

CHAPTER 7
A PERSONAL INTENSITY

1. Viktor Frankl, *Man's Search for Meaning* (Boston, MA: Beacon Press, 2006).

2. *Saving Private Ryan*, directed by Steven Spielberg (Hollywood, CA: Dreamworks Video, 1999), DVD.

3. From Winston Churchill's address to the House of Commons on June 4, 1940, "We Shall Fight on the Beaches," http://www.winstonchurchill.org/learn/speeches/speeches-of-winston-churchill/128-we-shall-fight-on-the-beaches (accessed September 18, 2014).

4. As quoted in *The Book of Military Quotations*, ed. Peter G. Tsouras (St. Paul, MN: Zenith, 2005), 216; citing Major-General Carl von Clausewitz, *On War*, 1832, trans. Michael Howard and Peter Paret, 1976.

5. Tremper Longman III, "The God of War," *Christianity Today* (May 2003), 62.

6. Don Terry, "US Army Open Inquiries Into Ranger Deaths," *New York Times*, February 18, 1995, http://www.nytimes.com/1995/02/18/us/army -opens-inquiries-into-ranger-deaths.html (accessed July 21, 2014).

7. US Army website "Soldier's Creed," http://www.army.mil/values/ soldiers.html (accessed July 21, 2014).

8. Bob Moorehead, "Rwandan Man's Confession," http://www .wayofthemaster.com/confession.shtml (accessed September 9, 2014).

CHAPTER 8
AN UNFLAGGING OPTIMISM

1. "Commander Howell M. Forgy, USN (ChC), (1908–1972)," Department of the Navy—Navy Historical Center, http://www.history.navy.mil/photos/ pers-us/uspers-f/h-forgy.htm (accessed July 21, 2014).

2. Samuel Adams, "An Oration Delivered at the State House, in Philadelphia," August 1, 1776 (printed in Philadelphia; reprinted in London for J. Johnson, 1776), 22.

3. Thomas Paine, "The Crisis," no. 1 in *The American Crisis*, series of pamphlets, 1776–1783, The Thomas Paine Library at LibertyOnline, http:// libertyonline.hypermall.com/Paine/Crisis/Crisis-TOC.html (accessed September 18, 2014).

4. Winston Churchill, "Never Give In," WinstonChurchill.org, http:// www.winstonchurchill.org/learn/speeches/speeches-of-winston-churchill/ 103-never-give-in (accessed September 18, 2014).

5. Jim McGuiggan, "I Will Do More than Live," in *Jesus, Hero of Thy Soul* (West Monroe, LA: Howard, 1998).

6. Ibid.

7. As recounted by Charles Swindoll in *Joseph: A Man of Integrity and Forgiveness* (Nashville, TN: Thomas Nelson, 1998). Viewed online at Google Books.

8. McGuiggan, "I Will Do More than Live," in *Jesus, Hero of Thy Soul*, citing Lloyd John Ogilvie, *The Bush Is Still Burning* (Waco, Texas: Word Books, 1980), 101–102.

9. Quote widely attributed to John Wayne. John W. Whitehead, "John Wayne Was *True Grit*," HuffingtonPost.com, June 6, 2011, http://www .huffingtonpost.com/john-w-whitehead/john-wayne-was-true-grit_b_871965 .html (accessed July 22, 2014).

10. As quoted by Henderson, *Stonewall Jackson and the American Civil War*, vol. 1, 200.

11. Library of Congress, "George Washington Papers at the Library of Congress, 1741-1799," http://www.loc.gov/teachers/classroommaterials/

connections/george-washington/langarts.html (accessed September 18, 2014).

12. Finkel, *The Good Soldiers,* 92.

13. G. K. Chesteron, *The Autobiography of G. K. Chesterton* (San Francisco: Ignatius Press, 2006; original ed., 1936), 217.

14. Finkel, *The Good Soldiers,* 101–102.

15. Rajiv Chandrasekaran, "Kasparov Proves No Match for Computer," *Washington Post,* May 12, 1997, http://www.washingtonpost.com/wp-srv/tech/analysis/kasparov/kasparov.htm (accessed July 22, 2014).

16. The author has adapted somewhat the NASB translation for Psalm 139.

CHAPTER 9
A DEEP CAMARADERIE

1. As quoted in Karel Montor, *Naval Leadership: Voices of Experience,* 481.

2. Marlantes, *What It Is Like to Go to War,* 175.

3. Malcolm MacPherson, *Roberts Ridge: A Story of Courage and Sacrifice on Takur Ghar Mountain, Afghanistan* (New York: Delacorte, 2005), 43–44.

4. Mansfield, *The Faith of the American Soldier,* 101.

5. Michael Norman, *These Good Men: Friendships Forged From War* (New York: Crown, 1989), 293.

6. *Band of Brothers,* directed by David Frankel and Tom Hanks (Los Angeles: HBO Studios, 2002), DVD.

CHAPTER 11
THE WARRIOR'S ETHICS

1. Carl von Clausewitz, *On War* (London: N. Trübner, 1873), trans. James John Graham, http://www.clausewitz.com/readings/OnWar1873/TOC.htm (accessed July 23, 2014).

2. US Army, "Ranger Creed," http://www.army.mil/values/ranger.html (accessed July 23, 2014).

3. Ibid.

4. See Alice Barr, "Man Says Apartment Complex Called His US Flag 'A Threat to Muslim Community,'" KHOU 11 News, June 18, 2014, http://www.khou.com/news/local/Man-says-apartment-complex-called-his-US-flag-a-threat-to-Muslim-community-263757051.html (accessed July 23, 2014); CBS Tampa Bay, "Vet Could Lose Home for Displaying Small US Flag in Front Yard Because It Violates Home Display Rules," June 26, 2014, http://tampa.cbslocal.com/2014/06/26/vet-could-lose-home-for-displaying-small-us-flag-in-front-yard-because-it-violates-home-display-rules/ (accessed July 23, 2014); CBS Los Angeles, "Soldiers' Mom Says She Was Told to Move

220

American Flag From Outside Home," June 20, 2014, http://losangeles
.cbslocal.com/2014/06/20/soldiers-mom-says-she-was-told-to-move
-american-flag-from-outside-home/ (accessed July 23, 2014).

5. CNN.com, "Ten Commandments Judge Removed From Office,"
November 14, 2003, http://www.cnn.com/2003/LAW/11/13/moore
.tencommandments/ (accessed July 23, 2014).

6. US Army, "75th Ranger Regiment: Being a Ranger," http://www
.goarmy.com/ranger/being-a-ranger.html (accessed September 18, 2014).

CHAPTER 12
JUST WAR

1. Michael Boylan, *Morality and Global Justice: Justifications and Applications* (Boulder, CO: Westview Press, 2011).

2. Dictionary.com, s.v., "combat," http://dictionary.reference.com/browse/
combat (accessed November 10, 2014).

3. Von Clausewitz, *On War.*

CHAPTER 13
THE GREATEST WARRIOR WHO EVER LIVED

1. Stu Weber, *Tender Warrior* (Sisters, OR: Multnomah, 1999), 264.

2. "If I Was Jesus," by Chuck Cannon and Phil Madeira. From the album
Shock'n Y'all, released by Dreamworks in 2003.

3. Weber, *Tender Warrior,* 264–265.

4. Lewis, *Mere Christianity,* 40–41.

CONNECT WITH US!

CHARISMA HOUSE

(Spiritual Growth)

 Facebook.com/CharismaHouse

@CharismaHouse

Instagram.com/CharismaHouse

SILOAM

(Health)

 **Pinterest.com/CharismaHouse**

MEV MODERN ENGLISH VERSION

(Bible)

www.mevbible.com